Unconditional Love: A Mother's Journey

While every precaution has been taken in the preparation of this book, the publisher assumes no responsibility for errors or omissions, or for damages resulting from the use of the information contained herein.

UNCONDITIONAL LOVE: A MOTHER'S JOURNEY

First edition. March 23, 2024.

Copyright © 2024 B Pily.

ISBN: 979-8224082261

Written by B Pily.

Table of Contents

Acknowledgments

I would like to express my heartfelt gratitude to everyone who contributed to the realization of this book. Special thanks to kmdestination for graciously allowing the use of their captivating image for the book cover. Your talent and generosity have added immeasurable beauty to this project.

I am also thankful to my family and friends for their unwavering support and encouragement throughout this journey. Your love and encouragement have been my guiding light.

To my readers, thank you for your interest in this book. I hope the words within these pages resonate with you and inspire you on your own journey of motherhood.

With deepest appreciation,

B Pily

About the Author

B Pily is a passionate writer who finds inspiration in the profound complexities of human relationships and the intricacies of the human experience. With a deep appreciation for the transformative power of storytelling, B Pily seeks to illuminate the beauty, resilience, and strength inherent in the bonds that connect us all.

Drawing from personal experiences, introspection, and a keen observation of the world around, B Pily crafts narratives that resonate with authenticity and sincerity. Through heartfelt prose and poignant reflections, B Pily invites readers to embark on a journey of self-discovery, empathy, and understanding.

"Unconditional Love: A Mother's Journey" is the culmination of B Pily's lifelong fascination with the timeless bond between mother and child. With a profound reverence for the maternal experience, B Pily weaves together stories, insights, and reflections that celebrate the enduring power of maternal love and the profound impact it has on our lives.

Beyond the written word, B Pily is a dedicated advocate for kindness, compassion, and social justice. Through storytelling and advocacy, B. Pily strives to create a more empathetic and inclusive world where every individual is valued, heard, and loved.

B Pily resides in Phura, where they continue to find inspiration in the beauty of nature, the richness of diverse cultures, and the resilience of the human spirit. When not writing, B Pily enjoys spending time with loved ones, exploring new horizons, and seeking moments of quiet contemplation amidst the hustle and bustle of life.

Dedication

Dedicated to all the mothers around the world,
whose love knows no bounds,
whose sacrifices are endless,
and whose strength is unmatched.
Your unwavering devotion and boundless affection
inspire us all to be better, do better, and love better.
This book is a tribute to your tireless efforts,
your selfless love, and your invaluable presence
in our lives.
Thank you for everything you do.

With love and gratitude,
B Pily

Preface

Dear Readers,

Welcome to "Unconditional Love: A Mother's Journey." This book is a heartfelt tribute to the enduring bond between mothers and their children, celebrating the profound love, sacrifices, and wisdom that define the essence of motherhood.

As someone who deeply appreciates the role of mothers in our lives, I have been inspired by the countless stories of maternal love and devotion that I've encountered. Each mother's journey is unique, yet there are universal themes of love, resilience, and selflessness that resonate across cultures and generations.

In "Unconditional Love: A Mother's Journey," we explore the multifaceted nature of motherhood, from the joys and triumphs to the challenges and sorrows. Through personal stories, reflections, and insights, we delve into the complexities of the maternal experience, honoring the resilience, strength, and unwavering love of mothers everywhere.

This book is dedicated to all the mothers who have touched our lives with their unconditional love and unwavering support. May their stories inspire and uplift you, reminding you of the profound impact that mothers have on shaping our lives and our world.

Thank you for embarking on this journey with me. I hope that "Unconditional Love: A Mother's Journey" will serve as a source of comfort, inspiration, and gratitude for all who appreciate the beauty of maternal love.

With love and appreciation,
B Pily

Introduction:

In the intricate tapestry of human experience, few bonds are as enduring and profound as that between a mother and her child. From the first flutter of life within the womb to the tender moments of nurturing and guidance, motherhood weaves a thread of unconditional love, resilience, and sacrifice that shapes our very existence.

In "Unconditional Love: A Mother's Journey," we embark on a heartfelt exploration of the multifaceted dimensions of motherhood. Through poignant stories, insightful reflections, and timeless wisdom, we celebrate the joys, navigate the challenges, and honor the profound impact of maternal love on our lives.

From the unparalleled bond forged in the crucible of childbirth to the tender moments of everyday nurturing, each chapter offers a glimpse into the complexities and beauty of the maternal experience. We delve into the depths of a mother's love, exploring its capacity to inspire, heal, and transform both parent and child alike.

As we journey through the pages of this book, let us pause to reflect on the extraordinary role that mothers play in shaping our identities, values, and aspirations. Let us honor their sacrifices, cherish their wisdom, and celebrate their unwavering devotion to the ones they hold dear.

May "Unconditional Love: A Mother's Journey" serve as a testament to the enduring power of maternal love—a love that knows no bounds and transcends all obstacles. May it inspire us to cherish the mothers in our lives, to nurture the bonds that unite us, and to embrace the profound beauty of the maternal journey.

With heartfelt gratitude and reverence,
B Pily

Defining Mother's Love

Motherhood is a journey unlike any other, characterized by boundless love, unwavering dedication, and profound sacrifice. It is a journey that begins with the miracle of birth, where a mother's heart is forever intertwined with that of her child. But beyond biology, motherhood transcends mere genetics; it is a state of being, a sacred bond that defies explanation.

At the heart of motherhood lies a love that knows no bounds—a love that is as vast as the oceans and as enduring as the stars. It is a love that is as gentle as a whisper in the night and as fierce as a lioness protecting her cubs. It is a love that is unconditional, unwavering, and unyielding in its devotion.

But what exactly is this elusive concept we call "mother's love"? It is more than just a feeling; it is a force of nature, an innate instinct that drives mothers to nurture, protect, and cherish their children above all else. It is a love that transcends time and space, surviving even in the face of life's greatest challenges.

In this book, we embark on a journey to explore the essence of mother's love—the tender moments, the sacrifices made, the lessons learned, and the legacy left behind. Through stories, reflections, and insights, we seek to unravel the mysteries of this profound bond and celebrate the extraordinary women who embody it.

Join us as we delve into the depths of motherhood, where love knows no limits and miracles abound. Together, let us honor the timeless beauty of mother's love and pay tribute to the remarkable women who shape our lives with their boundless compassion and unwavering devotion.

Chapter 1
The Miracle of Motherhood

"The influence of a mother in the lives of her children is beyond calculation."
- James E. Faust

Motherhood is a profound journey that begins long before a child takes their first breath, extending far beyond the moment of birth into the depths of the human experience. At its core lies the essence of creation, as mothers become the vessels through which life is brought forth into the world. Yet, motherhood is more than mere biology; it is a tapestry woven with threads of love, sacrifice, and profound connection.

Motherhood transcends the mere act of giving birth; it encompasses a myriad of roles, emotions, and responsibilities that shape the very fabric of human existence. At its essence, motherhood is an intricate tapestry woven with threads of love, sacrifice, nurturing, and resilience. It is a journey marked by profound transformations, both within oneself and in relation to others.

First and foremost, motherhood embodies the nurturing instinct—the innate desire to care for and protect one's offspring. From the moment a child is conceived, a mother's body becomes a sanctuary, providing warmth, nourishment, and sustenance for the growing life within. Throughout pregnancy, a mother's instincts kick in, guiding her to make choices that prioritize the well-being of her unborn child, even at the expense of her own comfort.

This nurturing instinct continues beyond childbirth, as mothers devote themselves wholeheartedly to the care and upbringing of their children. They serve as nurturers, educators, and emotional anchors, providing unwavering support and guidance through life's triumphs and tribulations. Whether it's soothing a crying baby in the middle of the night or offering words of encouragement during times of uncertainty, mothers possess an innate ability to comfort and uplift their children with a touch, a smile, or a kind word.

Furthermore, motherhood is characterized by selflessness and sacrifice—the willingness to put the needs of one's children above all else. Mothers make countless sacrifices, big and small, in order to provide their children with the best possible opportunities and experiences. They may sacrifice their own careers, dreams, and desires in order to ensure the happiness and success of their children. Whether it's foregoing personal luxuries to save money for their education or sacrificing sleep to tend to their needs, mothers demonstrate an unparalleled level of selflessness and devotion.

At the heart of motherhood lies an unbreakable bond—a bond that transcends words, actions, and even time itself. This bond is forged through countless shared experiences, from the first flutter of a baby's kick in the womb to the tearful goodbyes on the first day of school. It is a bond that grows stronger with each passing day, as mothers and children navigate life's ups and downs together, hand in hand.

In essence, motherhood is a journey of love—a journey that begins with the miracle of life and continues to unfold with each passing moment. It is a journey marked by joy, sorrow, laughter, and tears—a journey that challenges, inspires, and enriches the soul. And though the path may be fraught with obstacles and uncertainties, mothers walk it with unwavering determination, fueled by the boundless love that resides in their hearts.

The bond between a mother and child is one of the most profound and enduring relationships known to humanity. It is a bond that begins long before birth, as a mother nurtures and protects her child within the sanctuary of her womb. From the moment of conception, a deep and intimate connection is formed, characterized by a unique blend of biological, emotional, and spiritual ties.

During pregnancy, a mother and her unborn child share a symbiotic relationship unlike any other. As the child grows and develops, the mother's body provides everything they need for survival—nutrients, oxygen, protection—creating a bond that is as physical as it is emotional. Through the gentle rhythm of a mother's heartbeat and the soothing cadence of her voice, a profound sense of security and belonging is instilled within the child, laying the foundation for a lifelong bond.

This bond only deepens with the miracle of childbirth, as a mother holds her newborn child for the first time, awash with a flood of emotions—joy, wonder, and overwhelming love. In that moment, a sacred bond is forged, as the mother gazes into the eyes of her child and sees reflected back the purest essence of her own being. It is a bond that transcends words, a silent understanding that speaks volumes without the need for explanation.

As the child grows and matures, the bond between mother and child continues to evolve, shaped by countless shared experiences, moments of laughter and tears, triumphs and setbacks. Through the daily rituals of feeding, bathing, and bedtime stories, a mother nurtures and sustains her child, imparting wisdom, values, and unconditional love along the way.

But perhaps the true test of the mother-child bond lies in its resilience—the ability to weather life's storms and emerge stronger than before. In times of hardship and adversity, it is the comforting embrace of a mother's arms that provides solace and reassurance, a beacon of hope guiding her child through the darkest of nights.

Indeed, the bond between a mother and child is a force of nature, an unbreakable thread that weaves its way through the tapestry of human experience. It is a bond that transcends distance and time, remaining steadfast and unwavering in the face of life's challenges. And though the journey of motherhood may be fraught with ups and downs, joys and sorrows, one thing remains constant—the eternal bond between a mother and her child, a love that knows no bounds and endures for all eternity.

Unconditional love is perhaps one of the most powerful and profound forces in the universe—a force that transcends boundaries, defies logic, and touches the very essence of our humanity. It is a love that knows no bounds, no limitations, and no conditions—a love that is pure, unwavering, and eternal.

At its core, unconditional love is the essence of the human spirit—the driving force behind acts of kindness, compassion, and selflessness that define the human experience. It is the love that a parent feels for their child, regardless of their flaws or mistakes. It is the love that binds families together through life's trials and tribulations. It is the love that inspires acts of heroism and sacrifice, as individuals go above and beyond to help others in need.

In the context of motherhood, unconditional love takes on a special significance—a love that is both profound and transformative. From the moment of conception, a mother's love knows no bounds, as she nurtures and protects her child with a fierce and unwavering devotion. Through sleepless nights, countless sacrifices, and moments of joy and sorrow, a mother's love remains constant, a beacon of light guiding her child through life's journey.

But unconditional love is not limited to the bond between a mother and child; it extends to all facets of human relationships. It is the love that binds friends, partners, and communities together, fostering a sense of belonging, acceptance, and understanding. It is the love that transcends differences of race, religion, and culture, uniting us in our common humanity.

In this book, we explore the theme of unconditional love through the lens of motherhood—a journey marked by sacrifice, resilience, and boundless affection. Through stories, reflections, and insights, we delve into the profound impact of maternal love on individuals, families, and society as a whole. Join us as we celebrate the transformative power of unconditional love and honor the extraordinary women who embody it with grace, courage, and unwavering devotion.

Chapter 2
Embracing Motherhood
"Motherhood: All love begins and ends there."
- Robert Browning

Becoming a mother is a journey filled with a multitude of emotions—excitement, anticipation, fear, and overwhelming joy. It marks the beginning of a new chapter in one's life, a chapter that is as rewarding as it is challenging. From the moment a woman discovers she is expecting, to the day she holds her newborn in her arms, the journey of embracing motherhood is a rollercoaster ride of experiences, both exhilarating and daunting.

One of the first challenges that many expectant mothers face is the physical and emotional changes that come with pregnancy. From morning sickness and fatigue to mood swings and hormonal fluctuations, the journey of pregnancy can be physically and emotionally demanding. However, amidst the discomfort and uncertainty, there is also a sense of wonder and awe as the miracle of life unfolds within the womb. Feeling the first flutter of movement, seeing the baby's tiny heartbeat on an ultrasound, and watching the belly grow are all moments of joy that make the journey of pregnancy truly magical.

As the due date approaches, expectant mothers may also grapple with fears and anxieties about labor and delivery. The pain and uncertainty of childbirth can be daunting, but so too is the anticipation of finally meeting the little one who has been growing inside for nine months. With the support of loved ones, healthcare providers, and birthing classes, many mothers find the strength and courage to face childbirth with determination and resilience.

The moment of birth itself is a culmination of months of anticipation and preparation—a moment that is both exhilarating and overwhelming. From the first cry of the newborn to the first touch of their tiny fingers, the experience of holding one's child for the first time is indescribable. It is a moment filled with a flood of emotions—joy, relief, gratitude, and overwhelming love—as the realization sets in that a new life has entered the world, forever changing the course of one's own life.

But the journey of motherhood does not end with childbirth; rather, it is just beginning. In the days, weeks, and months that follow, new mothers navigate the challenges of sleepless nights, feeding schedules, and diaper changes, all while adjusting to their new role and responsibilities. It is a time of immense joy and bonding as mothers and babies get to know each other, learning to communicate and connect in their own unique way.

Through the challenges and joys of becoming a mother, women discover the depth of their own strength, resilience, and capacity for love. It is a journey of self-discovery and transformation—one that is marked by moments of triumph, moments of doubt, and moments of sheer wonder at the miracle of life. And though the road may be bumpy at times, the reward of embracing motherhood is immeasurable—the profound privilege of nurturing and shaping a new life, and the boundless love that comes with it.

The arrival of a newborn into the world marks the beginning of a sacred journey of nurturing and care—a journey that is both instinctual and deeply rewarding for mothers. From the moment a mother holds her newborn in her arms, she is propelled by an innate desire to provide love, comfort, and protection, ensuring that her child thrives and flourishes in the world.

One of the primary ways in which mothers nurture and care for their newborns is through breastfeeding. Breast milk is often referred to as "liquid gold" for its unparalleled nutritional benefits and immune-boosting properties. It contains the perfect blend of nutrients, antibodies, and enzymes tailored specifically to meet the needs of a growing infant. Not only does breastfeeding provide essential nourishment for the newborn, but it also fosters a unique bond between mother and child, as they engage in the intimate act of nursing. The physical closeness and skin-to-skin contact during breastfeeding promote feelings of security and attachment, laying the foundation for a strong mother-child bond.

Beyond breastfeeding, mothers attend to their newborns' physical needs with meticulous care and attention to detail. This includes changing diapers promptly, ensuring the baby is clean and dry, and dressing them in comfortable, weather-appropriate clothing. Bath time becomes a special bonding ritual, as mothers gently wash their baby's delicate skin while singing soft lullabies or engaging in playful conversation. Mothers also prioritize their newborn's sleep, creating a peaceful and soothing environment conducive to rest and relaxation.

In addition to meeting their newborn's physical needs, mothers provide emotional nurturing that is essential for their child's overall well-being. Through gentle touches, soothing words, and loving gazes, mothers communicate their unconditional love and affection to their newborns. They respond to their baby's cries with empathy and compassion, instinctively knowing how to comfort and soothe them in times of distress. Mothers create a safe and nurturing environment where their child feels loved, valued, and secure, fostering a sense of trust and attachment that is vital for healthy development.

As the days and weeks pass, mothers continue to nurture and care for their newborns, adapting to their ever-changing needs and milestones. They engage in activities that stimulate their baby's development, such as tummy time to strengthen their neck and upper body muscles, singing lullabies to soothe and calm them, and reading bedtime stories to encourage language development and cognitive skills. Mothers also prioritize their own well-being, recognizing that self-care is essential for being the best possible parent to their child. This may involve seeking support from partners, family members, or healthcare professionals, as well as finding time for rest, relaxation, and personal interests.

Through their unwavering dedication and selflessness, mothers provide a nurturing foundation upon which their newborns can thrive. They are the embodiment of love, sacrifice, and resilience, shaping the lives of their children with every cuddle, kiss, and whispered lullaby. And though the journey of motherhood may be challenging at times, the reward of watching their child grow and flourish under their care is immeasurable—a testament to the power of a mother's love.

The transition to motherhood is a profound and life-altering experience, marked by a myriad of changes, challenges, and joys. From the moment a woman becomes a mother, her world is forever transformed as she takes on the role of caregiver, nurturer, and protector of her newborn child. While the journey of motherhood is filled with moments of love and wonder, it is also accompanied by a period of adjustment as women navigate the complexities of their new role and responsibilities.

One of the first challenges that mothers face is the physical recovery from childbirth. Whether delivering vaginally or via cesarean section, the body undergoes significant changes during pregnancy and childbirth, and it takes time to heal and regain strength. Mothers may experience postpartum discomfort, fatigue, and hormonal fluctuations as their bodies adjust to the demands of motherhood. It is essential for mothers to prioritize self-care during this time, listening to their bodies and seeking support from healthcare providers, partners, and family members as needed.

In addition to physical recovery, mothers must also adapt to the emotional and psychological changes that accompany motherhood. The transition to motherhood can be overwhelming as women grapple with a range of emotions, including joy, anxiety, fear, and self-doubt. Many new mothers experience the "baby blues," a temporary period of mood swings and tearfulness that occurs in the days and weeks following childbirth. For some women, these feelings may evolve into postpartum depression or anxiety, requiring professional support and intervention. It is important for mothers to recognize the importance of self-care and mental health during this vulnerable time, seeking help and support when needed.

As mothers adjust to their new role, they also face the challenge of balancing their own needs and desires with the demands of caring for a newborn. The relentless cycle of feeding, changing diapers, and soothing a crying baby can leave mothers feeling overwhelmed and exhausted, with little time for self-care or personal interests. Finding time for rest, relaxation, and self-care becomes essential for maintaining physical and emotional well-being. This may involve enlisting the help of partners, family members, or trusted caregivers to provide support and assistance with childcare, allowing mothers to take breaks and recharge as needed.

Another aspect of adjusting to motherhood involves navigating the shifting dynamics of relationships with partners, family members, and friends. The arrival of a newborn can strain relationships as couples adjust to their new roles as parents and negotiate the division of labor and responsibilities. It is important for partners to communicate openly and honestly, expressing their needs and concerns while also offering support and understanding to one another. Family and friends can also play a crucial role in providing emotional support and practical assistance to new mothers, easing the transition to parenthood and alleviating feelings of isolation or loneliness.

As mothers settle into their new role and responsibilities, they begin to develop their own unique parenting style and approach. They draw upon their own experiences, values, and instincts to make decisions about feeding, sleep, discipline, and childcare. While seeking advice and support from trusted sources can be helpful, ultimately, mothers must trust their own judgment and intuition as they navigate the complexities of parenthood.

In conclusion, adjusting to the new role and responsibilities of motherhood is a journey filled with challenges, uncertainties, and moments of profound joy. It is a time of physical, emotional, and psychological transformation as women transition into their roles as mothers and caregivers. Through self-care, support from loved ones, and trust in their own instincts, mothers can navigate this period of adjustment with grace, resilience, and a deep sense of love and commitment to their newborn child.

Chapter 3
Mother's Sacrifice:
A Portrait of Selflessness

"The heart of a mother is a deep abyss at the bottom of which you will always find forgiveness."
- Honoré de Balzac

Motherhood is synonymous with sacrifice—a testament to the profound love and devotion that mothers have for their children. From the moment of conception, mothers embark on a journey of selflessness, willingly putting their own needs and desires aside to prioritize the well-being and happiness of their family.

One of the most profound sacrifices mothers make is the sacrifice of time. From the earliest days of infancy, mothers devote countless hours to meeting their child's needs, often at the expense of their own rest and relaxation. Whether it's feeding, changing diapers, or comforting a fussy baby in the middle of the night, mothers are always on call, ready to provide comfort and care to their little ones. As children grow older, mothers continue to invest their time in nurturing and supporting their development, attending school events, extracurricular activities, and doctor's appointments, all while juggling household responsibilities and, for many, professional obligations.

Financial sacrifice is another hallmark of motherhood. Mothers often prioritize their children's needs and wants above their own, stretching their budgets and making do with less to provide for their family. They may forego personal luxuries and indulgences, choosing instead to invest in their children's education, healthcare, and enrichment activities. Mothers may also sacrifice their careers or professional aspirations to stay home and care for their children, sacrificing potential income and career advancement for the sake of their family's well-being.

Emotional sacrifice is perhaps the most profound and enduring sacrifice that mothers make. From the moment of conception, mothers form a deep and unbreakable bond with their children, a bond that transcends words, actions, and even time itself. Mothers experience the full spectrum of emotions—joy, fear, anxiety, and love—as they navigate the challenges and triumphs of motherhood. They put their own needs and desires aside to prioritize the emotional well-being of their children, offering unconditional love, support, and guidance through life's ups and downs.

Mothers also make sacrifices in their relationships and personal pursuits for the sake of their children. They may put their own dreams and aspirations on hold to support their children's goals and ambitions, sacrificing their own desires for the sake of their family's happiness and success. Mothers also make sacrifices in their relationships with partners, family members, and friends, as they prioritize the needs of their children above all else.

The sacrifices that mothers make for their children are a testament to the depth of their love and devotion. From the mundane tasks of daily caregiving to the more significant decisions that shape the course of their children's lives, mothers willingly put their own needs aside to ensure the well-being and happiness of their family. Through their selflessness and sacrifice, mothers inspire us all, reminding us of the profound power of maternal love.

Examples of selfless acts of love by mothers abound, reflecting the boundless devotion and unwavering commitment they have for their children. These acts, both big and small, showcase the extraordinary lengths to which mothers will go to ensure the well-being and happiness of their families. Here are some poignant examples:

1. Sacrificing personal time: Mothers often sacrifice their own leisure time and personal interests to prioritize the needs of their children. They may forgo hobbies, social outings, or relaxation in order to spend quality time with their family, attend to their children's needs, or support their children's activities and interests.

2. Putting children's needs first: Mothers consistently prioritize the needs of their children above their own. This can manifest in various ways, such as ensuring their children have nutritious meals even if it means skipping their own, sacrificing sleep to comfort a sick or restless child, or giving up personal opportunities to support their children's endeavors.

3. Career sacrifices: Many mothers make significant sacrifices in their careers to accommodate the demands of motherhood. Some may choose to take breaks from their careers or reduce their work hours to be more available for their children. Others may pass up on career advancement opportunities or higher-paying jobs to prioritize their family's needs.

4. Advocating for their children: Mothers are fierce advocates for their children, tirelessly championing their rights and interests. They may navigate complex systems and bureaucracies to secure educational accommodations for children with special needs, advocate for fair treatment in school or social settings, or fight for access to necessary resources and support services.

5. Providing emotional support: Mothers offer unwavering emotional support to their children through life's challenges and triumphs. They provide a listening ear, a shoulder to cry on, and words of encouragement during difficult times. Mothers instill confidence, resilience, and a sense of self-worth in their children, serving as their steadfast pillars of strength.

6. Making personal sacrifices for their children's futures: Mothers make countless sacrifices to ensure their children have access to opportunities for growth and success. This may include investing financially in their children's education, sacrificing their own career aspirations to support their children's pursuits, or relocating to provide a better environment for their family.

7. Modeling selflessness and empathy: Above all, mothers lead by example, demonstrating the values of selflessness, compassion, and empathy to their children. Through their own actions and behaviors, mothers teach their children the importance of caring for others, giving back to their community, and making a positive impact in the world.

These examples represent just a fraction of the countless acts of selfless love and sacrifice that mothers demonstrate every day. Mothers are the unsung heroes of our lives, whose boundless love and dedication shape us into the individuals we become. Their sacrifices may often go unnoticed or unacknowledged, but their impact reverberates throughout our lives, leaving an indelible mark on our hearts and souls.

Chapter 4
The Strength of a Mother
"A mother is a woman who shows you the light when you just see the dark."
- Grimaldos Robin

Motherhood is not only a journey of love and joy but also one of resilience and determination. Mothers demonstrate extraordinary strength as they navigate the challenges and adversities that life presents, drawing upon their inner resources to overcome obstacles and emerge stronger than ever before. In this chapter, we explore the indomitable spirit of mothers, their unwavering resilience, and their remarkable ability to face adversity with grace and courage.

Resilience is a defining characteristic of motherhood. Mothers encounter a multitude of challenges, from sleepless nights and parenting struggles to personal setbacks and life's unexpected twists and turns. Despite these obstacles, mothers possess an inner strength that enables them to bounce back from adversity, to persevere in the face of hardship, and to find hope and resilience in even the darkest of times.

One of the most profound demonstrations of a mother's resilience is seen in her ability to weather the storms of life while remaining steadfast in her love and commitment to her children. Mothers face a myriad of challenges, from financial difficulties and health concerns to relationship struggles and personal crises. Yet, they find the strength to keep going, to put one foot in front of the other, and to continue providing love, support, and stability for their children, no matter the circumstances.

Determination is another hallmark of motherhood. Mothers are fiercely determined to create a better future for their children, to overcome obstacles and barriers, and to defy the odds stacked against them. They approach life with a sense of purpose and resolve, refusing to let setbacks or failures define their journey. Instead, they harness their determination to chart a course forward, to pursue their dreams, and to create a life filled with hope, possibility, and opportunity for their children.

The strength of a mother is perhaps most evident in her ability to transform adversity into growth and resilience. Mothers draw upon their experiences, their wisdom, and their unwavering faith to navigate life's challenges with grace and courage. They turn setbacks into opportunities, failures into lessons, and hardships into sources of strength. Through their resilience and determination, mothers inspire us all to face life's challenges with courage, to never give up hope, and to believe in the power of love to overcome even the greatest of obstacles.

The strength of a mother is a testament to the indomitable spirit of womanhood. Through their resilience and determination, mothers demonstrate the power of love to conquer adversity, to overcome obstacles, and to emerge stronger and more resilient than ever before. Their unwavering commitment to their children, their unyielding resolve in the face of hardship, and their boundless capacity for love and sacrifice serve as a beacon of hope and inspiration for us all.

Motherhood is a journey filled with challenges, obstacles, and unexpected twists and turns. From financial struggles and health concerns to personal crises and relationship difficulties, mothers encounter a myriad of hardships along the way. Yet, despite these challenges, mothers demonstrate extraordinary resilience and determination as they navigate life's ups and downs for the sake of their children.

Financial challenges are a common obstacle that many mothers face. From single mothers struggling to make ends meet to families grappling with job loss or economic instability, financial hardships can create significant stress and strain on families. Mothers often find themselves juggling multiple jobs, cutting expenses, and making difficult decisions to provide for their children's needs. They may sacrifice their own wants and desires, forgoing luxuries and comforts to ensure their children have food on the table, a roof over their heads, and access to essential resources and opportunities.

Health concerns are another obstacle that mothers may encounter on their journey of motherhood. Whether it's their own health issues or those of their children, mothers must navigate the complexities of healthcare systems, treatment options, and emotional turmoil. Mothers may face chronic illnesses, disabilities, or mental health challenges, requiring them to muster all their strength and resilience to care for themselves and their families. They become advocates for their children's health, tirelessly seeking answers, resources, and support to ensure their children receive the best possible care and treatment.

Personal crises and relationship difficulties can also present significant challenges for mothers. Whether it's coping with the loss of a loved one, navigating a divorce or separation, or facing other personal hardships, mothers must find ways to maintain stability and support for their children amidst turmoil and upheaval. They draw upon their inner strength and determination to provide comfort, reassurance, and stability for their children during difficult times, shielding them from the full impact of adversity while fostering resilience and hope for the future.

Despite the obstacles they face, mothers persevere with unwavering determination for the sake of their children. They find creative solutions, seek support from loved ones and community resources, and draw upon their faith and inner resilience to overcome challenges and forge a path forward. Mothers demonstrate incredible courage, sacrifice, and resilience as they navigate life's challenges, always with their children's best interests at heart.

The journey of motherhood is not without its challenges, but mothers face adversity with remarkable strength and determination for the sake of their children. Whether it's overcoming financial struggles, health concerns, personal crises, or relationship difficulties, mothers demonstrate extraordinary resilience as they navigate life's ups and downs. Their unwavering commitment to their children's well-being serves as a powerful testament to the depth of maternal love and the indomitable spirit of motherhood.

Stories of maternal strength and courage are as diverse and inspiring as the mothers who live them. These narratives exemplify the remarkable resilience, determination, and love that mothers embody in the face of adversity. Here are some poignant examples:

1. The Single Mother's Sacrifice: Sarah, a single mother of two, lost her husband unexpectedly to a tragic accident. Left to raise her children alone, she faced immense challenges, both emotionally and financially. Despite the overwhelming grief and hardship, Sarah displayed unwavering strength and courage as she worked tirelessly to provide for her family. She took on multiple jobs, sacrificed her own needs, and leaned on her support network for guidance and encouragement. Sarah's resilience and determination inspired her children to persevere through their loss and adversity, teaching them the value of resilience and perseverance in the face of life's challenges.

2. The Mother Battling Illness: Emily, a devoted mother of three, was diagnosed with cancer at a young age. Faced with the daunting prospect of treatment and uncertainty about her future, Emily approached her illness with remarkable courage and grace. Throughout her chemotherapy and surgeries, she remained steadfast in her determination to be there for her children, offering them love, support, and reassurance during their time of need. Emily's resilience and positive outlook served as a source of inspiration for her family and friends, demonstrating the power of love and hope in overcoming adversity.

3. The Refugee Mother's Journey: Maria, a refugee mother fleeing war and conflict in her homeland, embarked on a perilous journey with her children in search of safety and security. Despite facing unimaginable hardships and dangers along the way, Maria remained steadfast in her resolve to protect her children and provide them with a better future. She endured long days of travel, hunger, and uncertainty, drawing upon her inner strength and faith to guide her family to safety. Maria's courage and resilience in the face of adversity inspired others to persevere in the face of hardship and adversity.

4. The Mother Overcoming Addiction: Anna, a mother struggling with addiction, found the strength and courage to overcome her demons for the sake of her children. Faced with the devastating impact of her substance abuse on her family, Anna made the courageous decision to seek help and embark on the journey to recovery. Through sheer determination and unwavering commitment, she overcame her addiction, rebuilt her life, and became a source of inspiration and hope for her children. Anna's story serves as a powerful reminder of the transformative power of love and resilience in overcoming life's greatest challenges.

5. The Mother Fighting for Justice: Maria, a mother of one, found herself in a relentless battle for justice after her daughter became a victim of bullying at school. Despite facing resistance from school authorities and the community, Maria refused to back down, determined to hold those responsible accountable and ensure the safety of all children. She tirelessly advocated for anti-bullying measures, raised awareness about the issue, and fought for policy changes to protect vulnerable students. Maria's unwavering determination and courage sparked a movement in her community, inspiring others to stand up against injustice and create a safer environment for children everywhere. Her resilience and commitment to her daughter's well-being serve as a powerful reminder of the transformative impact of a mother's love and advocacy in creating positive change.

These stories of maternal strength and courage illustrate the remarkable resilience, determination, and love that mothers embody in the face of adversity. Through their unwavering commitment to their children and their indomitable spirit, mothers inspire us all to persevere in the face of life's challenges and to embrace the power of love, hope, and resilience in overcoming adversity.

Chapter 5
Unconditional Love

"A mother's love is unconditional, timeless, and eternal. It is a bond that transcends all barriers and withstands the tests of time."

- Unknown

Unconditional love is the cornerstone of motherhood, a bond that transcends time, circumstance, and imperfection. In this chapter, we delve into the profound depth and power of a mother's love, exploring how it is unwavering and enduring, and the myriad expressions of love and affection that define the maternal relationship.

A mother's love knows no bounds—it is deep, boundless, and all-encompassing. From the moment a child is conceived, a mother's heart expands with an overwhelming sense of love and devotion. This love is unconditional, unbreakable, and unconditional, transcending any shortcomings or imperfections. It is a love that is as infinite as the universe, capable of weathering any storm and conquering any obstacle in its path.

A mother's love is a force of nature, nurturing and sustaining her children through life's joys and sorrows. It is a love that celebrates triumphs and milestones, comforts and consoles during times of sadness and uncertainty, and provides unwavering support and encouragement through every stage of life's journey. A mother's love is a constant presence, a guiding light that illuminates the darkest of days and fills the heart with warmth and hope.

The depth and power of a mother's love are profound and multifaceted, encompassing a range of emotions, actions, and experiences that shape the maternal bond. At its core, a mother's love is an unparalleled force that defies description, transcending words and boundaries to touch the very essence of the human spirit.

1. Unconditional Acceptance: A mother's love embodies unconditional acceptance in numerous ways, manifesting in the following aspects:

1. *Acceptance of Individuality:* A mother's love celebrates the unique individuality of each child, embracing their personality traits, quirks, strengths, and weaknesses without judgment or comparison. Regardless of societal expectations or external standards, a mother accepts her children for who they are, recognizing their inherent worth and dignity as individuals.

2. *Non-Judgmental Support:* A mother's love provides a safe and non-judgmental space for her children to express themselves authentically, without fear of criticism or rejection. Whether it's sharing their dreams, struggles, or insecurities, children can trust that their mother will listen with an open heart and offer unconditional support and understanding.

3. *Forgiveness and Grace:* A mother's love extends forgiveness and grace, recognizing that her children are human and prone to making mistakes. Instead of holding grudges or dwelling on past errors, a mother offers forgiveness and guidance, helping her children learn from their experiences and grow into better individuals.

4. *Unconditional Presence:* A mother's love is characterized by unconditional presence, offering unwavering support and companionship through life's ups and downs. Whether it's celebrating achievements or providing comfort during times

of sorrow, a mother is always there for her children, offering a steady presence that reassures and strengthens them.

5. ***Unconditional Affection:*** A mother's love expresses affection and warmth unconditionally, showering her children with hugs, kisses, and expressions of love regardless of their behavior or circumstances. This affectionate touch reaffirms the bond between mother and child, fostering a sense of security and belonging that is essential for emotional well-being.

6. ***Empowerment and Encouragement:*** A mother's love empowers and encourages her children to embrace their true selves and pursue their passions and dreams. Instead of imposing her own aspirations or expectations onto her children, a mother nurtures their interests, talents, and ambitions, empowering them to explore their potential and follow their own path in life.

7. ***Unconditional Protection:*** A mother's love encompasses unconditional protection, ensuring the safety and well-being of her children at all costs. Whether it's shielding them from physical harm, defending them from bullies, or providing a nurturing environment that fosters emotional resilience, a mother's love is a powerful force that safeguards her children's welfare.

In summary, a mother's love demonstrates unconditional acceptance in its myriad forms, encompassing acceptance of individuality, non-judgmental support, forgiveness and grace, unconditional presence, affection, empowerment, and protection. Through these expressions of love, a mother creates a nurturing and supportive environment where her children can thrive and flourish, secure in the knowledge that they are unconditionally accepted and cherished for who they are.

2. Infinite Capacity: The depth of a mother's love knows no bounds—it is infinite in its capacity to nurture, protect, and support her children. From the moment of conception, a mother's heart expands to encompass the entirety of her child's existence, creating a bond that is as enduring as it is profound. Here's a deeper exploration of how a mother's love embodies this concept:

1. *Expansiveness of Heart:* A mother's love knows no bounds—it expands to accommodate the ever-changing needs and circumstances of her children. Like a vast ocean, her love is deep, wide, and expansive, capable of encompassing all aspects of her children's lives with warmth, compassion, and devotion.

2. *Endless Well of Compassion:* A mother's love is like an endless well of compassion, overflowing with empathy, understanding, and kindness. It is a wellspring of unconditional support and comfort that her children can draw from whenever they are in need, providing solace and strength in times of struggle or distress.

3. *Inexhaustible Reservoir of Strength:* A mother's love is a source of boundless strength and resilience, empowering her to face life's challenges with courage and grace. It is a reservoir of inner fortitude that enables her to weather storms, overcome obstacles, and navigate the complexities of parenthood with unwavering determination and resolve.

4. *Limitless Capacity for Sacrifice:* A mother's love is characterized by a limitless capacity for sacrifice, as she willingly gives of herself for the sake of her children's happiness and well-being. From the moment of conception, a mother devotes herself wholeheartedly to the care and nurturing of her children, making countless sacrifices along the way without hesitation or reservation.

5. *Eternal Nature:* A mother's love transcends the boundaries

of time and space, enduring long after her children have grown and forged their own paths in life. It is a love that remains eternally present, spanning generations and leaving an indelible mark on the hearts and souls of her descendants for all time.

6. ***Unconditional Support:*** A mother's love provides unwavering support and encouragement, fostering an environment where her children can thrive and flourish. It is a foundation of stability and security that empowers her children to pursue their dreams, overcome obstacles, and reach their full potential with confidence and determination.

7. ***Ever-Present Guidance:*** A mother's love offers ever-present guidance and wisdom, serving as a beacon of light that illuminates her children's paths and guides them through life's twists and turns. It is a compass that points them in the direction of truth, integrity, and compassion, instilling values and principles that shape their character and define their destiny.

In essence, a mother's love is characterized by its infinite capacity to nurture, protect, and support her children throughout every stage of their lives. It is a love that knows no limits, transcending the boundaries of human understanding to touch the very essence of the human spirit with its boundless warmth, compassion, and devotion.

3. Selfless Sacrifice: Selfless sacrifice is a cornerstone of a mother's love, demonstrating her unwavering commitment to the well-being and happiness of her children above all else. This aspect of maternal love is characterized by acts of profound selflessness, where a mother willingly puts her children's needs and interests ahead of her own, often at great personal cost. Here's a detailed exploration of selfless sacrifice in the context of a mother's love:

- ***Putting Children's Needs First:*** A mother's love compels her to prioritize her children's needs above her own desires or interests. From the moment of their birth, a mother instinctively dedicates herself to meeting her children's physical, emotional, and psychological needs, ensuring their health, safety, and happiness are paramount.

- ***Sacrificing Sleep and Rest:*** One of the most common forms of selfless sacrifice is sacrificing sleep and rest to care for a newborn or attend to the needs of growing children. Sleepless nights, round-the-clock feedings, and soothing a crying baby are all part of a mother's daily routine, as she puts aside her own need for rest to ensure her child's comfort and well-being.

- ***Putting Career Aspirations on Hold:*** Many mothers willingly put their career aspirations on hold or make significant adjustments to their professional goals to prioritize their family's needs. Whether it's taking a hiatus from work to care for young children, reducing work hours to accommodate family responsibilities, or sacrificing career advancement opportunities to be present for their children, mothers often make significant sacrifices in their professional lives for the sake of their families.

- ***Financial Sacrifices:*** A mother may make financial sacrifices to ensure her children have access to the resources and opportunities they need to thrive. This could involve budgeting carefully, foregoing personal luxuries, or making lifestyle adjustments to prioritize saving for her children's education, extracurricular activities, or future aspirations.

- ***Personal Sacrifices:*** A mother's love may also manifest in personal sacrifices she makes to ensure her children's happiness and well-being. This could involve giving up hobbies or personal interests to spend more time with her children, making compromises in her own social life or relationships to accommodate family commitments, or putting aside her own desires to support her children's dreams and ambitions.

- ***Emotional Sacrifices:*** A mother may also make emotional sacrifices for the sake of her children, setting aside her own worries, fears, and insecurities to provide a stable and nurturing environment for her family. This could involve putting on a brave face during challenging times, offering words of reassurance and encouragement, or shielding her children from the full impact of her own struggles and hardships.

- ***Acts of Service and Kindness:*** Selfless sacrifice is often demonstrated through everyday acts of service and kindness that mothers perform for their children without expecting anything in return. Whether it's cooking nutritious meals, helping with homework, providing emotional support during difficult times, or simply being there to listen and offer guidance, mothers continually give of themselves to ensure their children's needs are met and their hearts are filled with love and warmth.

Selfless sacrifice is a defining characteristic of a mother's love, reflecting her unwavering commitment to the well-being and happiness of her children above all else. Through acts of profound selflessness, mothers demonstrate the depth of their love and devotion, creating a nurturing and supportive environment where their children can thrive and flourish.

4. Unwavering Devotion: Unwavering devotion is a cornerstone of a mother's love, embodying her steadfast commitment to the care, nurturing, and well-being of her children. It is a deeply rooted and enduring aspect of maternal love, characterized by unwavering dedication and loyalty that transcends the trials and tribulations of life.

Here's a detailed exploration of unwavering devotion in the context of a mother's love:

- **Wholehearted Dedication:** A mother's love is defined by her wholehearted dedication to her children, as she devotes herself tirelessly to meeting their needs and ensuring their happiness and well-being. From the moment of their birth, a mother's devotion knows no bounds, as she selflessly commits herself to the lifelong journey of nurturing, guiding, and supporting her children through every stage of their lives.
- **Consistent Presence:** Unwavering devotion is demonstrated through a mother's consistent presence and availability to her children, providing a sense of security and stability that serves as a foundation for their growth and development. Whether it's being there to celebrate achievements, offer comfort during times of distress, or simply share in the everyday moments of life, a mother's unwavering presence is a constant source of reassurance and support.
- **Steadfast Support:** A mother's love is characterized by steadfast support, as she stands by her children through life's challenges and triumphs, offering unwavering encouragement, guidance, and advocacy. Whether it's helping with homework, cheering them on at sporting events, or providing a listening ear during moments of doubt or uncertainty, a mother's unwavering support reinforces her children's confidence and resilience in the face of adversity.
- **Emotional Stability:** Unwavering devotion is reflected in a mother's emotional stability and resilience, as she remains a source of strength and comfort for her children during times of uncertainty and upheaval. Through her unwavering love and commitment, a mother provides a sense of security and calmness that helps her children navigate life's challenges with courage and grace.

- ***Sacrificial Giving:*** A mother's devotion is often demonstrated through sacrificial giving, as she willingly sacrifices her own needs, desires, and aspirations for the sake of her children's happiness and well-being. Whether it's giving up personal time, making financial sacrifices, or setting aside her own dreams to prioritize her children's needs, a mother's unwavering devotion is exemplified in her selfless acts of giving and sacrifice.
- ***Long-Term Investment:*** Unwavering devotion is a long-term investment in the future of her children, as a mother dedicates herself wholeheartedly to shaping their lives and guiding them toward their fullest potential. Through her unwavering love and commitment, a mother instills values, imparts wisdom, and provides the support and encouragement her children need to thrive and succeed in life.
- ***Enduring Legacy:*** A mother's unwavering devotion leaves an enduring legacy that transcends generations, shaping the lives of her children and influencing the course of their descendants for years to come. Through her unwavering love and commitment, a mother leaves an indelible mark on the hearts and souls of her children, instilling in them a sense of purpose, resilience, and compassion that carries forward throughout their lives.

Unwavering devotion is a defining characteristic of a mother's love, reflecting her steadfast commitment to the care, nurturing, and well-being of her children. Through her unwavering love and commitment, a mother creates a foundation of strength and support that empowers her children to thrive and flourish, enriching their lives with a sense of security, stability, and unconditional love.

5. Boundless Empathy: Boundless empathy is a fundamental aspect of a mother's love, reflecting her deep capacity to connect with her children on an emotional level and provide them with the understanding and support they need to navigate life's ups and downs. Here's a more detailed exploration of boundless empathy in the context of a mother's love:

- *Sensitive Observation:* A mother's boundless empathy begins with sensitive observation and attunement to her children's emotions, thoughts, and needs. Through attentive listening and observation, she tunes into their nonverbal cues, subtle expressions, and changes in behavior, allowing her to discern their underlying feelings and concerns even when they may not be able to articulate them.

- *Validation and Understanding:* Boundless empathy is demonstrated through a mother's ability to validate and understand her children's experiences, emotions, and perspectives without judgment or criticism. Whether it's celebrating their triumphs, acknowledging their disappointments, or empathizing with their struggles, a mother's empathetic response communicates acceptance, validation, and support, fostering a sense of emotional validation and connection in her children.

- *Comfort and Reassurance:* A mother's boundless empathy extends to providing comfort and reassurance to her children during times of distress or uncertainty. Through her empathetic presence and nurturing touch, she offers solace, warmth, and safety, creating a secure and nurturing environment where her children can find refuge and support in the face of life's challenges.

- **Encouraging Emotional Expression:** Boundless empathy encourages emotional expression and vulnerability in her children, creating a safe and nonjudgmental space for them to share their thoughts, feelings, and experiences openly and honestly. Whether it's expressing joy, sadness, anger, or fear, a mother welcomes her children's emotional expression with empathy and compassion, validating their experiences and helping them develop emotional resilience and self-awareness.

- **Teaching Empathy:** A mother's boundless empathy serves as a model for her children, teaching them the importance of empathy, compassion, and kindness in their relationships with others. Through her own empathetic responses and interactions, she demonstrates the value of understanding and caring for others' feelings and perspectives, fostering empathy and emotional intelligence in her children that will serve them well throughout their lives.
- **Fostering Self-Discovery:** Boundless empathy creates a nurturing environment that fosters self-discovery and personal growth in her children. By empathizing with their experiences, challenges, and aspirations, a mother helps her children develop a deeper understanding of themselves, their values, and their goals, empowering them to navigate life's complexities with authenticity, confidence, and resilience.
- **Building Resilience:** Boundless empathy builds resilience in her children by providing them with the emotional support and validation they need to cope with adversity and bounce back from setbacks. Through her empathetic presence and unwavering support, a mother helps her children develop resilience, adaptability, and problem-solving skills, equipping them with the tools they need to thrive in an ever-changing world.

Boundless empathy is a cornerstone of a mother's love, enriching her children's lives with understanding, validation, and support. Through her empathetic response and nurturing presence, a mother creates a nurturing environment that fosters emotional growth, resilience, and self-discovery in her children, empowering them to navigate life's challenges with courage, compassion, and grace.

6. Eternal Connection: The concept of an eternal connection between a mother and child is deeply rooted in the enduring nature of maternal love, which transcends the boundaries of time, space, and even mortality. Here's a more detailed exploration of the eternal connection between a mother and child:

- *Transcending Physical Boundaries:* The bond between a mother and child is not limited by physical proximity or presence. Even when separated by distance or circumstances, the connection between them remains unbreakable, as their hearts remain intertwined across any expanse. This connection allows them to feel each other's love, support, and presence regardless of physical separation.
- *A Legacy of Love:* A mother's love leaves an indelible mark on the hearts and souls of her children, shaping their lives and influencing their choices long after she is gone. Even in death, a mother's love continues to exert a powerful influence, as her words of wisdom, acts of kindness, and expressions of love echo in the memories and hearts of her children, inspiring them to live with courage, compassion, and integrity.
- *Guiding Light:* A mother's love serves as a guiding light that illuminates her children's paths and helps them navigate life's complexities with grace and resilience. Even in moments of darkness or uncertainty, the memory of a mother's love provides comfort, reassurance, and guidance, empowering her children to overcome obstacles and pursue their dreams with confidence and determination.
- *Spiritual Connection:* The eternal connection between a mother and child often takes on a spiritual dimension, transcending the physical realm and touching the deepest

depths of the human spirit. Across cultures and belief systems, mothers are revered as sacred vessels of love and wisdom, embodying the divine qualities of nurturing, compassion, and unconditional love that connect all living beings in a web of interconnectedness and belonging.

- ***Continued Presence:*** Though a mother may no longer be physically present in her children's lives, her presence endures in the cherished memories, traditions, and values she imparted to them. Whether it's the scent of her perfume, the sound of her laughter, or the lessons she taught, a mother's presence lives on in the everyday moments and special occasions that her children hold dear, reminding them of her enduring love and influence.

- ***Honoring the Legacy:*** The eternal connection between a mother and child is honored through the preservation and celebration of her legacy. Whether through family traditions, rituals, or storytelling, children keep their mother's memory alive by passing down her teachings, values, and stories to future generations, ensuring that her love and wisdom continue to inspire and guide her descendants for years to come.

- ***Embracing the Continuum:*** Ultimately, the eternal connection between a mother and child reflects the cyclical nature of life and the interconnectedness of all beings in the grand tapestry of existence. Just as a mother's love endures beyond her physical presence, so too does the bond between generations, as each new life carries forward the love, lessons, and blessings bestowed upon them by those who came before.

The eternal connection between a mother and child is a testament to the enduring power of maternal love, which transcends time, space, and even mortality. Through the bond they share, mothers and children are united in a timeless continuum of love, wisdom, and grace that enriches their lives and shapes their destinies for generations to come.

7. **Transformative Influence:** The transformative influence of a mother's love is profound and far-reaching, shaping the very essence of her children's beings and guiding them along the paths of their lives. Here's a deeper exploration of how a mother's love imparts wisdom, strength, and resilience, empowering her children to navigate life's challenges with courage and grace:

- *Core Values and Beliefs:* A mother's love serves as the foundation upon which her children's values and beliefs are built. Through her words, actions, and teachings, she instills in them a moral compass and ethical framework that guides their decisions and shapes their character. Whether it's teaching the importance of honesty, compassion, integrity, or perseverance, a mother's love provides the guiding principles that inform her children's behavior and shape their interactions with the world around them.

- *Strength in Adversity:* A mother's love equips her children with the strength and resilience they need to weather life's storms and overcome adversity. Through her own example of perseverance and resilience in the face of challenges, she teaches her children the value of resilience, determination, and grit, empowering them to face setbacks with courage and optimism. Whether it's navigating personal hardships, academic challenges, or career setbacks, a mother's love provides a source of inner strength and fortitude that enables her children to rise above adversity and emerge stronger and wiser.

- *Emotional Intelligence:* A mother's love fosters emotional intelligence and self-awareness in her children, helping them understand and navigate their own emotions and those of others. Through her empathetic presence, active listening, and unconditional support, she creates a safe and nurturing environment where her children feel comfortable expressing their feelings and exploring their innermost thoughts. This emotional intelligence allows her children to develop healthy coping mechanisms, interpersonal skills, and empathy, empowering them to build meaningful relationships and navigate complex social dynamics with confidence and compassion.

- *Problem-Solving Skills:* A mother's love encourages critical thinking and problem-solving skills in her children, challenging them to approach life's challenges with creativity, resourcefulness, and resilience. Whether it's helping with homework, tackling household chores, or navigating interpersonal conflicts, a mother provides guidance and support that empowers her children to think critically, analyze situations, and find solutions that align with their values and goals. This problem-solving mindset prepares her children to face the uncertainties and complexities of adulthood with confidence and adaptability.

- *Sense of Identity and Purpose:* A mother's love nurtures her children's sense of identity and purpose, empowering them to embrace their unique talents, interests, and aspirations. Through her unconditional acceptance and encouragement, she fosters a sense of self-worth and confidence that allows her children to pursue their passions and dreams with conviction and enthusiasm. Whether it's pursuing academic excellence, exploring creative pursuits, or making a difference in their communities, a mother's love provides the affirmation and support her children need to pursue their passions and fulfill their potential.

The transformative influence of a mother's love is a powerful force that shapes the character and destiny of her children, instilling in them the values, beliefs, and principles that guide their lives. Through her unwavering love and guidance, a mother empowers her children to navigate life's challenges with courage, resilience, and grace, preparing them to embrace the opportunities and complexities of adulthood with confidence and determination.

In essence, the depth and power of a mother's love are incomprehensible, yet undeniably profound. It is a force that transcends the bounds of human understanding, infusing every aspect of a child's existence with warmth, security, and unconditional acceptance. Through its boundless capacity for love, sacrifice, and devotion, a mother's love remains the most enduring and influential force in shaping the human experience.

A mother's love is unwavering and enduring due to its inherent nature and the unique bond she shares with her children. Here's a detailed exploration of why a mother's love remains constant and unchanging over time:

1. **Unconditional Acceptance:** A mother's love is unconditional, meaning it is not contingent upon her children's actions, achievements, or behaviors. Regardless of any circumstances or challenges her children may face, a mother's love remains steadfast and unwavering, providing a consistent source of support and affirmation.

2. **Inherent Connection:** The bond between a mother and her child is deep-rooted and inherent, forged through the physical and emotional connection established during pregnancy and childbirth. This bond creates a strong foundation for a mother's love, which continues to grow and evolve throughout her children's lives, regardless of any external factors or changes.

3. **Protective Instinct:** A mother's love is often accompanied by

a strong protective instinct, driving her to safeguard her children from harm and ensure their well-being at all costs. This instinctual desire to nurture and protect her children fuels the unwavering nature of a mother's love, as she remains fiercely committed to their safety and happiness throughout their lives.

4. Emotional Investment:** A mother invests a significant amount of emotional energy and care into her children, forming deep emotional bonds that endure over time. This emotional investment creates a sense of attachment and commitment that transcends any obstacles or challenges, allowing a mother's love to withstand the test of time and adversity.

5. **Selflessness and Sacrifice:** A mother's love is characterized by selflessness and sacrifice, as she consistently puts her children's needs and well-being above her own. This willingness to prioritize her children's happiness and fulfillment demonstrates the enduring nature of a mother's love, as she remains dedicated to their care and support regardless of any personal sacrifices she may have to make.

6. **Consistent Presence:** A mother's love is marked by her consistent presence and availability to her children, providing a sense of stability and security that endures throughout their lives. Whether it's offering a listening ear, providing words of wisdom, or simply being there to offer a comforting hug, a mother's unwavering presence reinforces the enduring nature of her love and support.

7. **Legacy of Love:** A mother's love leaves a lasting legacy that continues to influence her children long after she is gone. The memories, values, and teachings she imparts serve as a timeless reminder of her love and devotion, shaping her children's lives and guiding their actions for generations to

come.

A mother's love is unwavering and enduring due to its unconditional nature, inherent connection, protective instinct, emotional investment, selflessness, consistent presence, and lasting legacy. Through thick and thin, in times of joy and sorrow, a mother's love remains a constant source of strength, support, and guidance for her children, shaping their lives and touching their hearts in A mother's love is a language of its own, spoken fluently through a myriad of gestures, actions, and expressions that convey her deep affection and unwavering devotion to her children. It is a love that transcends mere words, finding expression in the tender embrace of a hug, the gentle caress of a hand, and the warmth of a loving smile. In the quiet moments of everyday life, a mother's love is felt in the simple yet profound acts of care and attention that she showers upon her children.

From the earliest days of infancy, a mother's love is manifested in the nurturing touch of her hands as she cradles her newborn, soothing their cries and lulling them to sleep with the rhythm of her heartbeat. It is seen in the loving gaze she bestows upon her child, reflecting a depth of affection that words alone cannot express. As her children grow and mature, a mother's love evolves with them, adapting to their changing needs and circumstances while remaining steadfast and unwavering in its commitment.

Expressions of love and affection take many forms in a mother's daily interactions with her children. It may be found in the simple act of preparing a favorite meal, carefully crafted with love and attention to nourish both body and soul. It may be heard in the soft melodies of a lullaby sung at bedtime, offering comfort and reassurance in the darkness of the night. It may be felt in the gentle guidance and encouragement she provides as her children navigate the challenges of life, offering wisdom and support to help them find their way.

In addition to these everyday gestures of love, a mother's affection is often demonstrated through grander gestures of celebration and support. Whether it's cheering enthusiastically from the sidelines at a sports game, attending school performances with pride and admiration, or offering a shoulder to lean on during times of heartache and disappointment, a mother's love is a constant source of encouragement and support in both triumph and adversity.

Beyond the tangible expressions of love and affection, a mother's love is also conveyed through the intangible qualities of presence, acceptance, and understanding. It is found in the unwavering support she provides, the unconditional acceptance she offers, and the deep understanding she holds for her children's hopes, dreams, and aspirations. It is a love that knows no bounds, transcending distance and time to envelop her children in its warm embrace, even when they are far apart.

Ultimately, a mother's love is a force of nature, a powerful and enduring bond that shapes the lives of her children in profound and lasting ways. It is a love that enriches the soul, strengthens the spirit, and imbues life with meaning and purpose. In its infinite depth and boundless compassion, a mother's love is truly a gift beyond measure, a treasure to be cherished and celebrated for all eternity.

In conclusion, the chapter on "Unconditional Love" illuminates the profound and enduring nature of a mother's boundless affection and unwavering devotion to her children. Through a tapestry of gestures, actions, and expressions of care and devotion, a mother's love transcends the ordinary and elevates the human spirit to extraordinary heights. It is a love that knows no bounds, reaching across distance and time to envelop her children in its warm embrace, even in the face of life's greatest challenges and uncertainties.

From the tender moments of infancy to the triumphs and trials of adulthood, a mother's love remains a constant source of strength, support, and guidance. It is a love that celebrates achievements, comforts in times of sorrow, and empowers her children to navigate life's complexities with courage and grace. It is a love that endures beyond the physical realm, transcending life and death to leave an indelible mark on the hearts of her children for eternity.

As we reflect on the profound impact of a mother's love, we are reminded of its transformative power to shape lives, instill values, and inspire greatness. It is a love that embodies the very essence of humanity—compassionate, selfless, and eternal. In its infinite depth and boundless compassion, a mother's love is truly a testament to the beauty and resilience of the human spirit, a beacon of hope and comfort that illuminates our path and guides us on our journey through life.

Chapter: 6
Motherhood and Identity

"Motherhood is not only a biological identity; it is also a profound psychological and emotional journey that shapes who we are as individuals."

- Unknown

Motherhood is a transformative journey that holds the power to redefine a woman's sense of self, identity, and purpose. In this chapter, we delve into the intricate relationship between motherhood and identity, exploring how the experience of nurturing and caring for a child shapes a woman's understanding of herself and her place in the world.

At the heart of motherhood lies a profound sense of connection—a connection that extends beyond the physical bond between mother and child to encompass a deeper understanding of one's own strengths, vulnerabilities, and capacity for love. As women embark on the journey of motherhood, they undergo a process of self-discovery, growth, and transformation, embracing their roles as nurturers, caregivers, and mentors with grace and resilience.

Yet, alongside the joys and rewards of motherhood come challenges and complexities, particularly when it comes to balancing personal aspirations with the responsibilities of parenting. Women must navigate the delicate dance of prioritizing their own goals and ambitions while still nurturing the needs and well-being of their children. This balancing act requires courage, flexibility, and a willingness to embrace the ever-evolving nature of motherhood and identity.

In this chapter, we explore the multifaceted dimensions of motherhood and its profound impact on a woman's sense of self. From the identity shifts and challenges of reconciling personal aspirations with parenting responsibilities to the unparalleled opportunities for fulfillment and purpose that motherhood offers, we celebrate the transformative journey that is motherhood and the enduring legacy of love and resilience that it leaves in its wake. Join us as we embark on a journey of self-discovery, growth, and empowerment through the lens of motherhood and identity.

Shaping a Woman's Sense of Self:

Motherhood serves as a cornerstone of a woman's identity, intricately woven into the fabric of her being and shaping her self-perception, priorities, and values in profound ways. The journey of nurturing and caring for a child not only brings about external changes but also sparks internal transformations that redefine how a woman sees herself and her place in the world.

The experience of motherhood fosters a deeper understanding of one's strengths, vulnerabilities, and capacity for love. Through the joys and challenges of parenting, women are confronted with their own resilience, patience, and resourcefulness, revealing dimensions of themselves they may not have previously recognized. As they navigate the intricacies of raising a child, mothers discover new depths of empathy, compassion, and unconditional love within themselves, further enriching their sense of self and purpose.

In embracing their roles as nurturers, caregivers, and mentors, mothers undergo a profound transformation that extends beyond mere outward appearances. They learn to prioritize the well-being and happiness of their children above all else, reshaping their values and priorities to reflect the profound responsibility of parenthood. This shift in focus from self to other fosters a sense of selflessness and purpose that permeates every aspect of a woman's identity, guiding her actions and decisions with unwavering commitment and dedication.

Moreover, the challenges inherent in motherhood—from sleepless nights to the demands of balancing work and family life—serve as catalysts for personal growth and self-discovery. As mothers confront adversity and overcome obstacles, they cultivate resilience, adaptability, and strength of character that further shape their sense of self and identity. Each triumph and setback becomes a lesson in perseverance and courage, reinforcing their belief in their own capabilities and fortitude.

Ultimately, motherhood is a transformative journey that not only shapes a woman's sense of self but also empowers her to embrace her innate strengths, vulnerabilities, and capacity for love. Through the profound experience of nurturing and caring for a child, women discover new depths of resilience, compassion, and purpose within themselves, enriching their lives and leaving an enduring legacy of love and devotion for generations to come.

Balancing Personal Aspirations:

The journey of motherhood presents women with a delicate balancing act as they strive to reconcile their personal aspirations with the responsibilities of parenting. While the experience of motherhood brings immeasurable joy and fulfillment, it also necessitates sacrifices and compromises, especially when it comes to pursuing individual goals and ambitions.

Mothers often find themselves navigating a complex web of roles and responsibilities, from nurturing their children to managing household tasks and, in many cases, pursuing careers or other personal endeavors. This juggling act requires careful prioritization, time management, and a willingness to adapt to ever-changing circumstances.

At the heart of this balancing act lies the desire to fulfill both parental duties and personal aspirations without sacrificing the well-being and happiness of their children. Mothers are faced with the challenge of carving out time and space for their own pursuits while ensuring that their children's needs are met and their relationships remain strong and nurturing.

However, achieving this balance is no easy feat. Mothers may find themselves torn between competing demands, struggling to allocate time and energy effectively to both their children and their personal goals. They may experience feelings of guilt or inadequacy when they perceive themselves as falling short in either realm, leading to heightened stress and emotional strain.

Despite these challenges, mothers possess a remarkable capacity for resilience, adaptability, and resourcefulness. They learn to prioritize their time and efforts, setting boundaries and making choices that align with their values and priorities. They seek out support from partners, family members, and friends, recognizing the importance of community and collaboration in navigating the complexities of modern motherhood.

Moreover, mothers often discover unexpected sources of inspiration and motivation in their children, finding fulfillment and purpose in the act of nurturing and guiding their growth and development. The experience of motherhood may spark new creative passions, career aspirations, or personal interests, leading women to pursue their goals with renewed vigor and determination.

In navigating the delicate balance between personal aspirations and parenting responsibilities, mothers exemplify resilience, strength, and grace. They demonstrate an unwavering commitment to both their children and themselves, striving to create a life that is fulfilling, meaningful, and harmonious. Through their tireless efforts and unwavering dedication, mothers inspire us all to pursue our dreams while cherishing the precious moments of parenthood along the way.

Navigating Identity Shifts:

The transition to motherhood marks a profound shift in a woman's identity, as she navigates the complexities of reconciling her pre-existing sense of self with her new roles and responsibilities as a mother. This transformative process is both challenging and empowering, as women embark on a journey of self-discovery, growth, and personal evolution.

At the heart of this transition lies the need to reconcile conflicting aspects of identity—balancing the demands of parenthood with the desire to maintain a sense of individuality and self-expression. Mothers often grapple with feelings of identity loss or ambiguity as they adjust to their new roles, questioning their sense of identity and purpose in the face of profound life changes.

The process of navigating identity shifts involves introspection, reflection, and self-awareness as women explore the multifaceted dimensions of their identity and the roles they inhabit. Mothers may find themselves grappling with conflicting emotions and expectations, wrestling with the tension between their own desires and societal norms or expectations.

Yet, amidst the challenges of identity shifts, mothers discover unexpected sources of strength, resilience, and purpose. They embrace the opportunity for self-discovery and personal growth, recognizing the transformative power of motherhood to shape their sense of identity and purpose in profound ways.

In embracing their new roles as mothers, women find solace and fulfillment in the profound connection they share with their children. The experience of nurturing and caring for a child fosters a deep sense of belonging and purpose, anchoring mothers in a newfound sense of identity that transcends individual aspirations or achievements.

Moreover, the process of navigating identity shifts allows mothers to cultivate resilience, adaptability, and self-acceptance as they embrace the fluidity of identity and the ever-evolving nature of parenthood.

They learn to embrace the complexities of their identity, celebrating the unique blend of roles and responsibilities that define their experience as mothers.

Ultimately, the journey of navigating identity shifts in motherhood is one of growth, discovery, and empowerment. Through introspection, self-awareness, and a deepening connection with their children, mothers embrace the transformative power of parenthood to shape their sense of self and purpose in profound and meaningful ways. In navigating the complexities of identity shifts, mothers exemplify resilience, strength, and grace, inspiring us all to embrace the beauty and challenges of self-discovery and personal growth.

Finding Fulfillment and Purpose:

Despite the inherent challenges of balancing personal aspirations with the demands of parenting, motherhood offers unparalleled opportunities for fulfillment and purpose. The profound experience of nurturing and guiding a child through life's milestones is deeply rewarding, providing mothers with a sense of purpose and meaning that transcends individual achievements or accolades.

At the core of motherhood lies the transformative act of nurturing—a journey that unfolds in countless small moments of tenderness, care, and guidance. From the first tender embrace to the guiding hand through life's trials and triumphs, mothers play a pivotal role in shaping the lives of their children, instilling values, beliefs, and principles that guide them on their journey to adulthood.

In the act of nurturing, mothers find fulfillment not only in their own personal growth and accomplishments but also in the profound impact they have on shaping the lives of their children and future generations. Each milestone reached, each obstacle overcome, becomes a testament to the unwavering love and dedication of a mother, leaving an indelible mark on the hearts and minds of her children for years to come.

Moreover, the experience of motherhood fosters a deep sense of connection and belonging—a recognition that one's life is intertwined with the lives of their children in profound and meaningful ways. Mothers derive fulfillment from the bonds of love and affection they share with their children, finding purpose in the knowledge that their efforts are shaping the future and leaving a lasting legacy of love and compassion.

In motherhood, women discover a sense of purpose and meaning that transcends the pursuit of individual success or recognition. They find fulfillment not in accolades or achievements but in the simple joys of everyday life—the laughter of their children, the warmth of their embrace, the knowledge that they are making a difference in the lives of those they love most.

Ultimately, motherhood is a journey of selflessness, sacrifice, and profound love—a journey that offers unparalleled opportunities for fulfillment and purpose. In the act of nurturing and guiding their children, mothers find meaning in the knowledge that their love is shaping the future and leaving a legacy of compassion, kindness, and strength for generations to come. Through the profound experience of motherhood, women discover the true essence of fulfillment and purpose, embracing the beauty and challenges of parenthood with grace, resilience, and unwavering devotion.

Embracing the Journey:

Motherhood is not merely a destination but a transformative journey—a journey of self-discovery, growth, and transformation that challenges women to embrace the complexities of their identities and find balance amidst the demands of parenthood. It is a journey marked by both joy and sorrow, triumph and setback, as mothers navigate the ever-changing landscape of their roles and responsibilities.

At its core, motherhood is a journey of self-discovery—a process of uncovering layers of strength, resilience, and wisdom that lie dormant within. Through the challenges and triumphs of parenting, women come to know themselves in new and profound ways, tapping into reservoirs of courage and determination they never knew existed.

Moreover, motherhood is a journey of growth—a continuous evolution of mind, body, and spirit as women adapt to the ever-changing needs of their children and families. With each passing day, mothers learn and grow, gaining invaluable insights and experiences that shape their perspectives and priorities in profound and meaningful ways.

Yet, perhaps most importantly, motherhood is a journey of transformation—a journey that transcends individual aspirations and achievements to leave an enduring legacy of love, compassion, and strength. In embracing the joys and sorrows, triumphs and setbacks of parenthood, women discover a newfound sense of purpose and fulfillment that enriches their lives and shapes the legacy they leave behind.

Through the act of nurturing and guiding their children, mothers find meaning in the knowledge that their love is shaping the future and leaving a lasting imprint on the hearts and minds of those they hold dear. They embrace the challenges of parenthood with grace and resilience, knowing that each obstacle overcome is a testament to their unwavering devotion and commitment to their children.

In embracing the journey of motherhood, women find solace and strength in the knowledge that they are not alone—that they are part of a community of mothers who share in the joys and challenges of parenting. Together, they draw inspiration and support from one another, finding comfort and encouragement in the shared experience of raising the next generation.

Ultimately, motherhood is a journey that challenges women to embrace the complexities of their identities and find balance amidst the demands of parenthood. It is a journey that celebrates the resilience, strength, and unwavering love of mothers everywhere, leaving an indelible mark on the hearts and minds of generations to come.

In conclusion, the chapter on "Motherhood and Identity" explores the transformative journey of parenthood, where women navigate the complexities of their identities amidst the demands of raising children. Through the lens of motherhood, women embark on a journey of self-discovery, growth, and transformation, uncovering layers of strength, resilience, and purpose that shape the legacy they leave behind.

As women embrace the roles of nurturer, caregiver, and mentor, they redefine their sense of self, finding fulfillment and meaning in the profound connection they share with their children. Motherhood challenges women to reconcile their pre-existing identities with their new roles as mothers, leading to shifts in priorities, values, and perspectives that enrich their lives in profound and meaningful ways.

Despite the challenges of balancing personal aspirations with parenting responsibilities, motherhood offers unparalleled opportunities for growth and fulfillment. Through the joys and sorrows, triumphs and setbacks of parenthood, women discover a newfound sense of resilience, strength, and purpose that empowers them to embrace the journey with grace and determination.

Ultimately, motherhood is a transformative journey that celebrates the resilience, strength, and unwavering love of mothers everywhere. It is a journey that transcends individual aspirations and achievements, leaving an enduring legacy of compassion, kindness, and strength for generations to come. Through the profound experience of motherhood, women discover the true essence of their identities and the power of their love to shape the world around them.

Chapter 7

The Role of a Mother in Child Development

"The influence of a mother in the life of a child is unparalleled, shaping their development in profound ways from infancy through adulthood."

- Unknown

In the intricate tapestry of child development, the role of a mother stands as a cornerstone, shaping the emotional, social, and cognitive growth of her children in profound ways. From the earliest moments of infancy to the formative years of adolescence, mothers play a pivotal role in nurturing the potential and well-being of their children.

In this chapter, we delve into the multifaceted dimensions of the mother-child relationship, exploring the profound impact of a mother's love on the development of her children. Through responsive caregiving, affectionate touch, and attentive communication, mothers create a secure and loving environment that fosters emotional resilience, cognitive growth, and social competence.

We examine how mothers nurture emotional intelligence and resilience in their children, teaching them to recognize and regulate their emotions, navigate social interactions, and cope with life's challenges. Through their unconditional love and unwavering support, mothers empower their children to develop the skills and strengths they need to thrive in an ever-changing world.

Join us as we celebrate the invaluable role of mothers in shaping the development of their children and explore the enduring legacy of love, guidance, and nurturing care that mothers leave in the hearts and minds of their children for generations to come.

The Impact of a Mother's Love on Child Development:

A mother's love is the cornerstone of a child's emotional, social, and cognitive development, shaping their entire trajectory from infancy to adulthood. From the very first moments of life, a mother's nurturing presence lays the foundation for a child's sense of security and attachment, forming the bedrock upon which healthy relationships are built.

In the tender embrace of their mother, infants find solace and comfort, learning to trust in the world around them and forming secure attachments that serve as a blueprint for future relationships. Through responsive caregiving, mothers attune to their child's needs, providing comfort, nourishment, and reassurance in times of distress.

Affectionate touch, such as gentle caresses and warm hugs, communicates love and acceptance, reinforcing the bond between mother and child and promoting feelings of safety and belonging. In the nurturing cocoon of their mother's embrace, children learn to regulate their emotions, develop self-soothing skills, and form a secure internal foundation from which to explore the world.

Moreover, attentive communication is a cornerstone of a mother's love, providing children with the emotional support and validation they need to thrive. Through words of encouragement, praise, and affirmation, mothers bolster their children's self-esteem and confidence, instilling a sense of worthiness and belonging that extends far beyond childhood.

As children grow and develop, the impact of a mother's love continues to resonate, influencing their social interactions, cognitive abilities, and overall well-being. The secure attachment formed in infancy serves as a buffer against stress and adversity, fostering resilience and adaptive coping strategies that serve children well throughout their lives.

In essence, a mother's love is the nurturing force that propels children toward their full potential, imbuing them with the confidence, resilience, and emotional intelligence needed to navigate life's challenges with grace and resilience. Through their unwavering love and dedication, mothers lay the foundation for a lifetime of happiness, success, and meaningful relationships, leaving an enduring legacy of love that shapes the lives of their children for generations to come.

Nurturing Emotional Intelligence and Resilience:

Mothers are pivotal in nurturing emotional intelligence and resilience in their children, equipping them with essential skills to navigate the complexities of life with grace and strength. Through their own actions and interactions, mothers serve as powerful role models, demonstrating empathy, compassion, and self-regulation in their daily lives.

By modeling these qualities, mothers teach their children to recognize and express their emotions in healthy ways, laying the groundwork for emotional intelligence. Children learn to identify and articulate their feelings, developing a nuanced understanding of their emotional experiences and those of others. This heightened emotional awareness fosters empathy and compassion, enabling children to form deep, meaningful connections with others based on understanding and mutual respect.

Furthermore, through open communication and active listening, mothers create a safe and supportive environment where children feel valued and understood. By validating their children's emotions and experiences, mothers help them develop a sense of self-worth and confidence, empowering them to express themselves authentically and assertively.

In navigating complex social situations, mothers serve as guides and mentors, offering guidance and support as their children learn to navigate the intricacies of human relationships. Through patient coaching and gentle encouragement, mothers help their children develop the social skills and emotional resilience needed to navigate conflict, set boundaries, and build healthy, fulfilling relationships with others.

Moreover, mothers play a crucial role in helping their children cope with life's inevitable challenges and setbacks. By providing a listening ear, offering words of encouragement, and helping their children develop problem-solving skills, mothers instill a sense of resilience and resourcefulness that enables their children to bounce back from adversity with resilience and determination.

In essence, mothers are the architects of their children's emotional development, shaping the foundation upon which their social and psychological well-being are built. Through their nurturing presence, mothers empower their children to navigate life's ups and downs with confidence, compassion, and resilience, preparing them to thrive in a complex and ever-changing world.

Creating a Secure and Loving Environment for Growth:

At the heart of a mother's role is the creation of a secure and nurturing environment where children can thrive emotionally, socially, and intellectually. Through their unwavering love and dedication, mothers provide the stability and support that children need to develop confidence, autonomy, and a sense of belonging.

Central to this nurturing environment are consistent routines and clear boundaries, which provide children with a sense of structure and predictability. By establishing regular daily routines for activities such as meal times, bedtime, and play, mothers create a sense of stability and security that helps children feel safe and grounded.

Moreover, mothers offer unconditional love and acceptance, creating a safe space where children can express themselves freely and without judgment. Through their words and actions, mothers convey a message of love, warmth, and acceptance, instilling a deep sense of self-worth and belonging in their children.

In addition to providing emotional support, mothers play a crucial role in fostering intellectual growth and development in their children. Through engaging activities, stimulating conversations, and opportunities for exploration and discovery, mothers encourage their children to question, learn, and grow intellectually.

Furthermore, mothers serve as cheerleaders and encouragers, celebrating their children's successes and offering gentle guidance and support during times of challenge. By fostering a growth mindset and emphasizing the importance of effort and perseverance, mothers instill a sense of resilience and determination in their children that enables them to overcome obstacles and achieve their goals.

Ultimately, the nurturing home environment created by mothers serves as a fertile ground for children to reach their full potential and flourish in all aspects of life. Through their unwavering love, support, and guidance, mothers empower their children to navigate the world with confidence, compassion, and resilience, preparing them to thrive in an ever-changing and complex world.

Emotional Availability:

Mothers play a crucial role in fostering emotional well-being in their children by being emotionally available and attuned to their needs, feelings, and experiences. Emotional availability entails being present and responsive to children's emotional cues, creating a safe and nurturing space where they feel understood, supported, and valued.

One of the key aspects of emotional availability is active listening. Mothers actively listen to their children without judgment or interruption, giving them their full attention and validating their emotions. By empathizing with their children's feelings and experiences, mothers convey a message of acceptance and understanding, fostering a deep sense of connection and trust.

Moreover, mothers demonstrate empathy by putting themselves in their children's shoes and understanding the world from their perspective. This empathetic approach helps mothers respond to their children's emotional needs with compassion and sensitivity, strengthening the bond between them and promoting healthy emotional development.

Validation is another important aspect of emotional availability. Mothers validate their children's emotions by acknowledging their feelings and letting them know that it's okay to feel the way they do. This validation helps children develop a sense of self-worth and self-acceptance, empowering them to express themselves authentically and confidently.

In creating a nurturing space characterized by emotional availability, mothers lay the groundwork for healthy emotional development in their children. By fostering open communication, empathy, and validation, mothers empower their children to navigate their emotions with resilience and confidence, setting the stage for positive relationships and emotional well-being throughout life.

Consistent Discipline:

In addition to being nurturing and supportive, mothers also play a crucial role in providing consistent discipline to their children. Consistent discipline is essential for helping children learn boundaries, rules, and consequences, which are important for their overall development and well-being.

One aspect of consistent discipline is setting clear expectations. Mothers establish clear rules and guidelines for behavior, outlining what is acceptable and what is not. By communicating these expectations clearly and consistently, mothers provide children with a framework for understanding their role within the family and society.

Furthermore, mothers enforce appropriate consequences when children fail to meet these expectations. Consequences may vary depending on the situation and the child's age, but they should always be fair, reasonable, and consistent. By following through with consequences consistently, mothers help children understand the connection between their actions and the resulting outcomes.

Consistent discipline also helps children develop self-discipline and self-control. By experiencing predictable consequences for their actions, children learn to regulate their behavior and make responsible choices. Over time, this fosters a sense of internalized discipline, empowering children to act in accordance with rules and expectations even when no one is watching.

Moreover, consistent discipline teaches children the importance of respect for authority and consideration for others. By respecting the rules set by their mothers and accepting the consequences of their actions, children learn to respect authority figures and take responsibility for their behavior.

Overall, consistent discipline is essential for helping children develop self-discipline, responsibility, and respect for others. By setting clear expectations, enforcing appropriate consequences, and fostering self-control, mothers empower their children to navigate the complexities of the world with confidence and integrity.

Encouraging Independence:

Mothers play a vital role in nurturing independence in their children, empowering them to develop the skills and confidence needed to navigate the world with autonomy and self-reliance. By fostering a sense of autonomy and providing opportunities for growth, mothers help their children develop into capable and self-assured individuals.

One way mothers encourage independence is by assigning age-appropriate tasks and responsibilities. From a young age, children can take on simple chores such as tidying up their toys or setting the table. As they grow older, mothers gradually increase the complexity of tasks, allowing children to develop new skills and capabilities at their own pace.

Moreover, mothers empower children to make decisions and problem-solve independently. By offering guidance and support while allowing children to take the lead, mothers instill a sense of confidence and self-efficacy in their children. This hands-on approach to decision-making helps children develop critical thinking skills, resilience, and adaptability, preparing them to face challenges with confidence and resourcefulness.

Furthermore, mothers provide a supportive environment where children feel safe to explore and experiment. By offering encouragement and praise for their efforts, mothers bolster children's self-esteem and motivation to learn. This positive reinforcement reinforces children's belief in their own abilities and encourages them to embrace new challenges with enthusiasm and determination.

Ultimately, encouraging independence allows children to develop a sense of ownership and agency over their lives, fostering a strong sense of self-esteem and self-worth. By nurturing independence in their children, mothers empower them to become resilient, resourceful, and self-assured individuals capable of achieving their goals and navigating life's challenges with confidence and grace.

Cultivating Creativity:

Mothers play a vital role in nurturing creativity in their children, providing them with opportunities for artistic expression, imaginative play, and exploration. By fostering creativity, mothers empower children to think outside the box, express themselves authentically, and develop essential skills for problem-solving and innovation.

One way mothers cultivate creativity is by providing materials and opportunities for artistic expression. From a young age, children are encouraged to explore different art mediums such as drawing, painting, sculpting, and crafting. Mothers create a supportive environment where children feel free to experiment and express themselves creatively, without fear of judgment or criticism.

Furthermore, mothers encourage imaginative play, which allows children to explore their creativity in a fun and imaginative way. Whether it's playing dress-up, building forts, or creating imaginary worlds, mothers provide opportunities for children to use their imagination and creativity to engage in open-ended play. This type of play stimulates creativity, fosters problem-solving skills, and encourages children to think creatively and innovatively.

In addition to artistic expression and imaginative play, mothers also encourage storytelling and narrative exploration. Through storytelling, children have the opportunity to use their imagination to create characters, settings, and plots, fostering creativity and language development. Mothers may also engage in collaborative storytelling activities, where children contribute their own ideas and perspectives to create unique and imaginative stories together.

Moreover, mothers provide opportunities for exploration and discovery, both indoors and outdoors. Whether it's exploring nature, visiting museums, or experimenting with science experiments, mothers expose children to a variety of experiences that stimulate curiosity and creativity. By encouraging children to ask questions, make observations, and draw connections, mothers foster a sense of wonder and curiosity that fuels creative thinking and innovation.

Ultimately, by nurturing creativity in their children, mothers empower them to become imaginative, innovative, and resourceful individuals capable of thinking outside the box and finding creative solutions to life's challenges. Through artistic expression, imaginative play, storytelling, and exploration, mothers lay the foundation for a lifetime of creativity and innovation in their children.

Promoting Physical Health:

Mothers play a crucial role in promoting physical health in their children, ensuring they receive the nutrition, exercise, and rest needed to thrive physically, mentally, and emotionally. By prioritizing physical health, mothers instill lifelong habits that support overall well-being and vitality.

One way mothers promote physical health is by providing nutritious meals and snacks. Mothers ensure that children have access to a balanced diet rich in fruits, vegetables, whole grains, lean proteins, and healthy fats. By offering a variety of nutrient-dense foods, mothers support children's growth and development, as well as their immune function and energy levels.

Furthermore, mothers encourage regular physical activity as part of a healthy lifestyle. Whether it's playing outside, participating in sports, or engaging in active play indoors, mothers provide opportunities for children to move their bodies and stay active. Regular exercise not only promotes physical fitness and strength but also enhances mood, cognitive function, and overall well-being.

In addition to nutritious eating and regular exercise, mothers prioritize adequate rest and sleep for their children. Mothers establish consistent bedtime routines and create a calm and soothing sleep environment to promote restful sleep. Sufficient sleep is essential for children's physical growth and development, as well as their cognitive function, emotional regulation, and immune function.

Moreover, mothers model healthy habits and lifestyle choices for their children to emulate. By demonstrating behaviors such as eating balanced meals, exercising regularly, getting enough sleep, and managing stress effectively, mothers set a positive example for their children and instill healthy habits that can last a lifetime.

Ultimately, by prioritizing physical health, mothers lay the foundation for their children to lead healthy, active, and fulfilling lives. Through nutritious eating, regular exercise, adequate rest, and positive role modeling, mothers empower their children to take charge of their own health and well-being, setting them on a path toward lifelong vitality and resilience.

Fostering Social Connections:

Mothers play a crucial role in fostering social connections in their children, providing them with opportunities to interact positively with peers, family members, and community members. By facilitating social interactions and encouraging meaningful connections, mothers help children develop essential social skills, empathy, and a sense of belonging within their social networks.

One way mothers foster social connections is by arranging playdates and social outings for their children. Whether it's inviting friends over to play, arranging outings to parks or playgrounds, or participating in organized activities such as sports or arts classes, mothers create opportunities for children to interact with peers and develop social skills in a supportive and supervised environment.

Furthermore, mothers model positive social behaviors and interpersonal skills for their children to emulate. By demonstrating qualities such as kindness, empathy, cooperation, and respect in their own interactions with others, mothers teach children how to navigate social situations with grace and integrity. Through their example, mothers instill values of empathy, inclusivity, and kindness in their children, fostering a culture of positive social interaction and mutual respect.

In addition to fostering connections with peers, mothers also encourage children to develop strong bonds with family members and community members. By participating in family activities, celebrations, and traditions, mothers help children develop a sense of belonging and connection within their family unit. Similarly, by engaging with neighbors, community members, and local organizations, mothers expose children to diverse perspectives and experiences, broadening their social horizons and fostering a sense of community pride and belonging.

Moreover, mothers provide support and guidance as children navigate the complexities of social relationships. By offering advice, listening empathetically, and helping children problem-solve conflicts and misunderstandings, mothers empower children to build and maintain healthy, positive relationships with others.

Ultimately, by fostering social connections, mothers provide children with the social skills, empathy, and sense of belonging needed to thrive in their interpersonal relationships and navigate the complexities of the social world with confidence and resilience. Through their guidance and support, mothers lay the foundation for children to develop meaningful connections, build strong relationships, and lead fulfilling lives within their social networks and communities.

Celebrating Diversity:

Mothers play a pivotal role in celebrating diversity and promoting cultural understanding in their children, exposing them to a variety of cultures, traditions, and perspectives. By embracing diversity and teaching children to appreciate the richness of human differences, mothers foster empathy, tolerance, and inclusivity, preparing children to thrive in a diverse and interconnected world.

One way mothers celebrate diversity is by exposing their children to multicultural books, music, and art. By reading stories from diverse cultures, listening to music from around the world, and exploring art from different traditions, mothers introduce children to the beauty and richness of human diversity. Through these cultural experiences, children learn to appreciate the unique customs, beliefs, and values of people from diverse backgrounds, fostering empathy and understanding.

Furthermore, mothers engage children in cultural activities and celebrations that highlight the traditions and customs of different cultures. Whether it's attending cultural festivals, participating in community events, or preparing traditional foods from around the world, mothers provide children with opportunities to immerse themselves in diverse cultural experiences and learn about the world beyond their own.

In addition to exposing children to different cultures externally, mothers also foster cultural understanding and appreciation within the home. By sharing stories of their own cultural heritage, family traditions, and values, mothers help children develop a sense of pride and connection to their own cultural identity while also encouraging curiosity and respect for other cultures.

Moreover, mothers teach children the importance of empathy, tolerance, and inclusivity in their interactions with others. By modeling respectful behavior and language, challenging stereotypes and prejudices, and promoting open-mindedness and acceptance, mothers instill values of compassion and respect for diversity in their children, preparing them to be compassionate and inclusive members of society.

By celebrating diversity, mothers empower their children to embrace the richness of human differences, foster empathy and understanding, and build bridges across cultures and communities. Through their guidance and example, mothers help children develop the attitudes, skills, and values needed to thrive in a diverse and interconnected world, where respect for diversity is celebrated as a source of strength and enrichment for all.

In conclusion, the role of a mother in child development is multifaceted and essential for fostering healthy emotional, social, and cognitive growth in children. Through their unwavering love, support, and guidance, mothers lay the foundation for children to thrive emotionally, socially, and intellectually.

A mother's love provides the emotional security and validation that children need to develop a strong sense of self-worth and resilience. By being emotionally available and attuned to their children's needs, mothers create a nurturing environment where children feel understood, supported, and valued.

Moreover, mothers play a crucial role in nurturing emotional intelligence and resilience in their children. By modeling empathy, compassion, and self-regulation, mothers teach children to recognize and manage their emotions effectively, fostering healthy relationships and coping skills that serve them well throughout life.

Additionally, mothers create a secure and loving environment where children can explore, learn, and grow. Through consistent discipline, clear boundaries, and unconditional love, mothers provide the stability and support that children need to develop confidence, autonomy, and a sense of belonging.

Furthermore, mothers promote physical health by prioritizing nutritious eating, regular exercise, and adequate rest for their children. By modeling healthy habits and lifestyle choices, mothers instill a foundation of well-being that supports children's physical, mental, and emotional health.

Lastly, mothers foster social connections and celebrate diversity, exposing children to different cultures, traditions, and perspectives. By encouraging positive interactions with peers, family members, and community members, mothers help children develop social skills, empathy, and a sense of belonging within their social networks.

In essence, the role of a mother in child development is characterized by unconditional love, nurturing support, and unwavering dedication. Through their tireless efforts and boundless love, mothers shape the lives of their children in profound and lasting ways, laying the groundwork for a future filled with promise, resilience, and possibility.

Chapter 8

Celebrating Motherhood

"Motherhood: the most beautiful journey of love, sacrifice, and joy that enriches our lives and shapes our souls."

- Unknown

Motherhood is a sacred and revered institution that transcends boundaries of culture, geography, and time. It is a universal experience that binds humanity together, shaping the course of history and influencing the destiny of nations. At its core, motherhood embodies the essence of selflessness, compassion, and unconditional love, serving as a guiding light that illuminates the path of life's journey.

In this chapter, we embark on a journey to explore the multifaceted dimensions of motherhood and the profound impact it has on individuals, families, and societies. From honoring mothers and their contributions to society to celebrating the unique traditions and rituals associated with motherhood, we delve into the rich tapestry of maternal love and sacrifice that defines the human experience.

Join us as we pay tribute to the countless mothers around the world who have dedicated their lives to nurturing, supporting, and empowering the next generation. Through their boundless love and unwavering devotion, mothers shape the future and leave an indelible mark on the hearts and minds of those they touch.

Mothers are the unsung heroes of society, whose contributions often go unrecognized but are undeniably vital to the fabric of our communities. Their selfless dedication, boundless love, and unwavering sacrifice shape the very foundation upon which our societies thrive. From the moment a child is born, a mother's nurturing touch and unwavering support lay the groundwork for a lifetime of growth, learning, and success.

In addition to their roles as caregivers and nurturers, mothers are often active participants in the workforce, contributing their talents, skills, and expertise to various industries and sectors. Whether as professionals, entrepreneurs, or volunteers, mothers bring a unique perspective and invaluable contributions to the workplace, enriching the collective experience and driving innovation and progress.

Beyond their individual achievements, mothers play a pivotal role in shaping the next generation of leaders, innovators, and change makers. Through their guidance, mentorship, and example, mothers instill values of empathy, compassion, and resilience in their children, empowering them to make positive contributions to society and effect meaningful change in the world.

It is essential to honor and recognize the immeasurable impact of mothers on individuals, families, and communities. Their tireless efforts and boundless love lay the groundwork for a brighter future, inspiring us all to strive for excellence and to give back to the world with the same selflessness and dedication that defines motherhood.

Mother's Day Celebrations and Traditions Around the World:

Mother's Day is a universal celebration that honors the selfless love, care, and sacrifices of mothers worldwide. While the specific date and customs associated with Mother's Day may vary from country to country, the sentiment remains consistent—to express gratitude and appreciation for the maternal figures who enrich our lives with their unwavering love and support.

In many parts of the world, Mother's Day is celebrated on the second Sunday of May, following the tradition established in the United States by Anna Jarvis in the early 20th century. On this day, families come together to honor mothers through various expressions of love and appreciation.

In the early 20th century, a woman named Anna Jarvis embarked on a heartfelt mission to honor her own mother and all mothers around the world. Inspired by her mother's unwavering love and devotion, Anna tirelessly advocated for the establishment of a national day dedicated to celebrating motherhood. Her efforts bore fruit in 1914 when President Woodrow Wilson officially proclaimed the second Sunday in May as Mother's Day in the United States. Anna's poignant tribute to her mother sparked a global movement, spreading love and appreciation for mothers across continents and cultures. Today, we continue to honor Anna Jarvis's legacy by celebrating Mother's Day with heartfelt gestures of gratitude and love for the remarkable women who have shaped our lives with their boundless love and sacrifice.

One common tradition associated with Mother's Day is the giving of heartfelt cards, flowers, and gifts as tokens of gratitude and affection. These gestures symbolize the deep appreciation and love that individuals feel for their mothers, acknowledging the invaluable role they play in their lives.

In addition to gift-giving, Mother's Day often involves special outings and family gatherings, where mothers are treated to a day of relaxation, pampering, and quality time with their loved ones. Whether it's a leisurely brunch, a picnic in the park, or a heartfelt home-cooked meal, these moments of togetherness provide an opportunity for families to celebrate and cherish the bond between mothers and their children.

While Mother's Day is widely celebrated on the second Sunday of May, the date and customs may vary in different cultures and countries. For example, in the United Kingdom, Mother's Day, also known as Mothering Sunday, is celebrated on the fourth Sunday of Lent, while in countries like Mexico and Japan, Mother's Day is observed on fixed dates in May.

Regardless of the specific date or customs, Mother's Day serves as a poignant reminder of the profound impact mothers have on our lives and the importance of expressing gratitude and appreciation for their unconditional love and sacrifices. It is a time to honor and celebrate the remarkable women who have shaped our lives with their boundless love, wisdom, and guidance.

Recognizing the Importance of Maternal Figures in Our Lives:

While the role of a mother is often associated with biological ties, the influence of maternal figures extends far beyond bloodlines to encompass a diverse array of women who play nurturing roles in our lives. From grandmothers and aunts to stepmothers and mentors, these maternal figures serve as pillars of strength, wisdom, and support, enriching our lives with their boundless love and guidance.

Grandmothers, with their warmth and wisdom, offer a wealth of life experience and sage advice, providing a sense of continuity and connection to our family's history and heritage. Their unconditional love and unwavering support serve as a source of comfort and reassurance during life's triumphs and challenges.

Similarly, aunts play a special role in our lives, offering a unique blend of love, laughter, and companionship. Whether acting as confidantes, cheerleaders, or role models, aunts enrich our lives with their nurturing presence and unwavering support, shaping our identities and values in profound ways.

Stepmothers, too, play an important role in our lives, navigating the complexities of blended families with grace and compassion. Despite the challenges they may face, stepmothers offer love, stability, and acceptance, fostering a sense of belonging and unity within their families.

Beyond familial ties, maternal figures can also include mentors, teachers, and friends who offer guidance, encouragement, and inspiration. These women serve as role models and mentors, imparting valuable lessons and insights that shape our identities, values, and aspirations.

It is crucial to acknowledge and honor the profound influence these maternal figures have on shaping our lives. Their love, guidance, and support contribute to our growth and development, instilling values of compassion, resilience, and integrity that guide us on our journey through life. By recognizing the importance of maternal figures in our lives, we honor the diverse tapestry of women who enrich our world with their boundless love and nurturing spirit.

Motherhood as a Symbol of Unconditional Love:

Motherhood stands as an enduring testament to the boundless depths of unconditional love, illuminating the essence of selflessness and compassion inherent in the maternal bond. It embodies a love that transcends all barriers, surpassing the realms of time, space, and circumstance. From the moment of conception, a mother's heart swells with an unwavering devotion that knows no bounds, as she selflessly dedicates herself to the well-being and happiness of her child.

In the tender embrace of a mother's arms, there exists a sanctuary of solace and security, where her love serves as a beacon of light in life's darkest moments. With each nurturing touch and whispered lullaby, she imparts a sense of warmth and comfort that envelops her child in a cocoon of love and protection.

Mothers exemplify the epitome of sacrifice and devotion, willingly placing the needs of their children above their own. They labor tirelessly, day and night, to provide for their children's physical, emotional, and spiritual needs, often at great personal cost. Their love knows no bounds, extending beyond the realms of comprehension to encompass the entirety of their child's existence.

Through their unwavering devotion and selfless sacrifice, mothers embody a love that transcends all obstacles and hardships. It is a love that perseveres through life's trials and tribulations, steadfast and unyielding in the face of adversity. In their boundless affection and tender care, mothers offer a glimpse into the inherent goodness and compassion within humanity, inspiring us all to aspire to greater heights of love and empathy.

Across cultures and generations, the profound expression of maternal love resonates deeply within the hearts of individuals, serving as a beacon of hope and reassurance in a world often fraught with uncertainty. Motherhood stands as a timeless symbol of unconditional love, reminding us of the transformative power of compassion and selflessness to heal, uplift, and unite humanity in a bond of shared humanity.

At the heart of motherhood lies a love that transcends the limitations of human understanding—a love that is boundless, infinite, and eternal. It is a love that finds expression in the simplest of gestures—a tender caress, a loving smile, a whispered word of encouragement—yet holds the power to move mountains and conquer all obstacles.

Mothers exemplify the epitome of sacrifice and devotion, willingly placing the needs of their children above their own. They labor tirelessly, day and night, to provide for their children's physical, emotional, and spiritual needs, often at great personal cost. Their love knows no bounds, extending beyond the realms of comprehension to encompass the entirety of their child's existence.

Through their unwavering devotion and selfless sacrifice, mothers embody a love that transcends all obstacles and hardships. It is a love that perseveres through life's trials and tribulations, steadfast and unyielding in the face of adversity. In their boundless affection and tender care, mothers offer a glimpse into the inherent goodness and compassion within humanity, inspiring us all to aspire to greater heights of love and empathy.

Across cultures and generations, the profound expression of maternal love resonates deeply within the hearts of individuals, serving as a beacon of hope and reassurance in a world often fraught with uncertainty. Motherhood stands as a timeless symbol of unconditional love, reminding us of the transformative power of compassion and selflessness to heal, uplift, and unite humanity in a bond of shared humanity.

In the gentle embrace of a mother's love, we find solace and sanctuary, a haven of peace and serenity amidst life's storms. It is a love that knows no boundaries, crossing oceans and continents to reach its intended recipient. Whether through words spoken or deeds done, mothers express their love in myriad ways, each gesture a testament to the depth and magnitude of their affection.

As we reflect on the profound significance of motherhood, let us pause to honor and celebrate the remarkable women who embody the essence of unconditional love. Their selfless devotion, unwavering compassion, and boundless generosity inspire us to be better, to love more deeply, and to cherish each precious moment with those we hold dear. In the embrace of a mother's love, we find the truest expression of humanity's capacity for love, kindness, and compassion—a love that knows no bounds and endures for all eternity.

Legacy of Wisdom and Traditions Passed Down Through Generations:

Mothers stand as custodians of a rich tapestry of wisdom, traditions, and values that have been passed down through generations, weaving together the threads of past, present, and future. They carry within them the collective knowledge and experience of their ancestors, embodying the resilience, strength, and wisdom of those who came before them.

From ancestral teachings and cultural practices to family rituals and cherished memories, mothers play a vital role in preserving and perpetuating the legacy of their forebears. Through their words and actions, mothers impart the timeless wisdom and cherished traditions that have been handed down through generations, instilling a sense of continuity and connection to our shared heritage.

In the nurturing embrace of a mother's love, children learn not only the practical skills and knowledge passed down through the ages but also the deeper lessons of resilience, compassion, and integrity that define our human experience. Mothers serve as beacons of wisdom and guidance, offering insights and advice gleaned from years of lived experience, tempered by the trials and tribulations of life's journey.

Through their guidance and nurturing, mothers shape the identities and destinies of future generations, ensuring that the legacy of their ancestors endures for years to come. They instill in their children a reverence for tradition, a respect for cultural heritage, and a deep appreciation for the values that bind us together as a global community.

As we honor and celebrate the profound influence of mothers on our lives, let us also recognize the invaluable role they play in preserving and perpetuating the legacy of wisdom and traditions passed down through generations. Their love, guidance, and teachings serve as a bridge between past and present, connecting us to our roots and inspiring us to carry forward the torch of knowledge and wisdom for the benefit of generations yet to come.

Mothers serve as the storytellers of our family narratives, weaving together the threads of history, culture, and personal experience into a tapestry of shared identity. Through the retelling of family anecdotes, the passing down of cherished recipes, and the celebration of cultural festivals, mothers impart a sense of belonging and continuity that spans across generations. In preserving and sharing these stories, mothers ensure that the memories of our ancestors remain alive in our hearts and minds, serving as guiding lights on our own journeys through life.

Furthermore, mothers embody the spirit of resilience and adaptation, drawing strength from the lessons of the past to navigate the challenges of the present and shape the possibilities of the future. In the face of adversity, mothers rise to the occasion with grace and determination, demonstrating the power of perseverance and tenacity in overcoming obstacles. Their ability to evolve and adapt while staying true to their values and traditions serves as a source of inspiration for future generations, reminding us of the enduring legacy of courage, resilience, and hope passed down through the ages.

In conclusion, mothers stand as pillars of strength, wisdom, and love, weaving together the threads of past, present, and future to create a tapestry of unconditional love and enduring legacy. Throughout the chapters of this book, we have explored the multifaceted nature of motherhood, from the miraculous journey of childbirth to the profound impact of maternal love on child development, from the sacrifices and challenges mothers face to the joy and fulfillment they find in nurturing their children.

As we reflect on the themes of unconditional love, sacrifice, resilience, and legacy, we are reminded of the profound influence mothers have on shaping our lives and shaping the world around us. Their love knows no bounds, transcending time and space to leave an indelible mark on our hearts and souls. From the earliest moments of infancy to the twilight years of old age, mothers guide, support, and inspire us with their unwavering devotion and boundless compassion.

In honoring and celebrating mothers, we pay tribute to the countless women who have enriched our lives with their love, wisdom, and sacrifice. Their legacy lives on in the traditions, values, and memories they pass down through generations, shaping the fabric of our society and the destiny of humanity itself.

May we always cherish and appreciate the extraordinary gift of motherhood, recognizing the immeasurable impact mothers have on shaping our world with their love, resilience, and unwavering commitment to the well-being of their children. As we honor the legacy of maternal love and sacrifice, let us strive to embody the qualities of compassion, empathy, and selflessness that define the essence of motherhood, ensuring that their legacy endures for generations to come.

Chapter 9

Mother-Daughter Relationships

"The mother-daughter relationship is a dance of love, understanding, and forgiveness, a delicate balance of nurturing and independence that evolves with time."

- Unknown

The bond between a mother and daughter is one of the most profound and intricate relationships in human experience. It is a connection that transcends mere biology, encompassing shared experiences, emotions, and a deep-seated sense of kinship. From the moment of birth, mothers and daughters embark on a journey of discovery and growth, navigating the ebbs and flows of life together. In this chapter, we will delve into the unique dynamics of the mother-daughter relationship, exploring its complexities, challenges, and transformative power. Through candid reflections, personal anecdotes, and insightful analysis, we will uncover the essence of this extraordinary bond and examine the ways in which it shapes our identities, influences our choices, and enriches our lives. Join us as we embark on a journey to explore the multifaceted world of mother-daughter relationships and discover the profound depths of love, understanding, and connection that define this timeless bond.

Exploring the unique bond between mothers and daughters:

The relationship between a mother and daughter is a multifaceted and deeply intimate bond that transcends the boundaries of familial ties. It is a connection forged through shared experiences, mutual understanding, and unconditional love. From the moment of conception, mothers and daughters embark on a journey together, navigating the highs and lows of life with a bond that knows no bounds.

At its core, the mother-daughter bond is characterized by a profound sense of mutual understanding and empathy. Mothers possess an innate ability to anticipate their daughters' needs and emotions, while daughters often find solace and reassurance in the unwavering support of their mothers. This shared understanding forms the foundation of a relationship that evolves and matures over time, becoming richer and more complex with each passing year.

Throughout the chapters of our lives, mothers and daughters share a multitude of experiences that shape their relationship and strengthen their connection. From the tender moments of infancy, when a mother cradles her newborn daughter in her arms, to the challenges and triumphs of adulthood, when daughters turn to their mothers for guidance and wisdom, the bond between them deepens and matures with each passing milestone.

In this chapter, we will delve into the intricacies of the mother-daughter relationship, exploring the dynamics that define this special bond and examining the ways in which it shapes our identities and influences our lives. Through candid reflections, personal anecdotes, and insightful analysis, we will uncover the essence of this extraordinary relationship and celebrate the profound love, understanding, and connection that define the mother-daughter bond. Join us as we embark on a journey to explore the depths of this timeless and cherished relationship, discovering the beauty and complexity of the bond between mothers and daughters.

Navigating challenges and conflicts in the relationship:

Navigating challenges and conflicts in the mother-daughter relationship requires patience, understanding, and open communication. Despite the deep bond that exists between them, mothers and daughters are individuals with their own unique perspectives, personalities, and aspirations. As a result, disagreements and conflicts are inevitable as they navigate the complexities of their relationship.

One common source of conflict in mother-daughter relationships is the generation gap. Mothers and daughters often come from different cultural backgrounds, generations, and life experiences, which can lead to misunderstandings and clashes in values and beliefs. For example, a mother may have grown up in a different era with different societal norms and expectations, while her daughter may have been raised in a more progressive and modern environment. These differences in upbringing and worldview can create friction and tension between them, as they struggle to reconcile their perspectives.

Communication styles also play a significant role in fueling conflict within mother-daughter relationships. Each individual may have their own preferred way of expressing themselves and interpreting the words and actions of the other. For instance, a mother may tend to be more direct and assertive in her communication, while her daughter may prefer a more indirect or passive approach. These differences in communication styles can lead to misunderstandings and misinterpretations, escalating conflicts and hindering effective resolution.

Additionally, unresolved issues from the past can resurface and contribute to ongoing conflicts in the relationship. Whether stemming from childhood disagreements or more recent conflicts, unresolved issues can linger beneath the surface, festering over time and exacerbating tensions between mothers and daughters. Without proper resolution and closure, these unresolved issues can continue to strain the relationship and hinder its growth and development.

In navigating these challenges and conflicts, it is essential for both mothers and daughters to approach the relationship with empathy, patience, and understanding. By actively listening to each other's perspectives, expressing themselves honestly and respectfully, and seeking to find common ground, they can work through their differences and strengthen their bond. Through open and honest communication, they can address underlying issues, heal past wounds, and build a relationship based on mutual respect, trust, and love.

Furthermore, the transition from childhood to adolescence and adulthood introduces a host of new challenges that can strain the mother-daughter relationship. As daughters assert their independence and seek to establish their own identities, conflicts over autonomy and boundaries may arise. Mothers, accustomed to nurturing and guiding their children, may struggle to relinquish control and adapt to their daughters' evolving needs for independence and self-expression. These power struggles can create friction within the relationship as both parties navigate the delicate balance between fostering autonomy and maintaining a sense of parental authority.

Moreover, external factors such as societal expectations and cultural influences can also impact the dynamics of the mother-daughter relationship and contribute to conflicts. For example, societal pressures to conform to traditional gender roles or cultural norms may place additional strain on the relationship as mothers and daughters navigate conflicting expectations and values. Additionally, life transitions such as marriage, career changes, or relocation can disrupt the dynamic between mothers and daughters, requiring them to renegotiate their roles and boundaries in light of these changes.

In navigating these challenges and conflicts, it is crucial for mothers and daughters to approach the relationship with empathy, patience, and a willingness to compromise. By acknowledging and validating each other's perspectives, they can build mutual respect and understanding, even in the face of disagreement. Through open and honest communication, they can address underlying issues and work together to find constructive solutions. Ultimately, by fostering a relationship built on trust, empathy, and mutual support, mothers and daughters can navigate the challenges of their relationship with grace and resilience, strengthening their bond and enriching their lives in the process.

Building a strong and supportive mother-daughter connection:

Building a strong and supportive mother-daughter connection is essential for nurturing a healthy and fulfilling relationship. While conflicts and challenges may arise, fostering a deep bond based on trust, empathy, and mutual respect can help mothers and daughters weather any storm and emerge stronger together.

One key aspect of building a strong mother-daughter connection is open and honest communication. Encouraging an environment where both parties feel comfortable expressing their thoughts, feelings, and concerns fosters understanding and strengthens their relationship. By actively listening to each other without judgment and communicating openly and respectfully, mothers and daughters can bridge the gap between them and forge a deeper connection.

Additionally, spending quality time together is vital for strengthening the mother-daughter bond. Whether it's sharing a meal, engaging in a favorite activity, or simply having a heartfelt conversation, carving out time for meaningful interactions helps nurture closeness and intimacy. These shared experiences create lasting memories and deepen the bond between mothers and daughters, fostering a sense of connection and belonging.

Moreover, showing appreciation and support for each other is essential for building a strong mother-daughter connection. Expressing gratitude for the love, guidance, and sacrifices made by mothers, and acknowledging the unique strengths and qualities of daughters cultivates mutual respect and admiration. By celebrating each other's achievements, offering encouragement during challenging times, and being each other's biggest cheerleaders, mothers and daughters can create a supportive and nurturing environment where they feel valued and cherished.

Furthermore, setting healthy boundaries and respecting each other's autonomy is crucial for maintaining a strong mother-daughter connection. Recognizing and honoring each other's individuality, preferences, and personal space fosters independence and self-expression while preserving the integrity of the relationship. Respecting boundaries ensures that both parties feel heard, understood, and respected, laying the foundation for a healthy and balanced relationship.

Here are five additional paragraphs to further explore the topic of building a strong and supportive mother-daughter connection:

1. **Shared Values and Beliefs:** Building a strong mother-daughter connection often involves identifying and embracing shared values and beliefs. When mothers and daughters align on fundamental principles and priorities, it strengthens their bond and provides a solid foundation for their relationship. Whether it's a commitment to honesty, integrity, compassion, or resilience, having common values fosters mutual understanding and reinforces their connection.

2. **Mutual Empowerment:** A strong mother-daughter connection involves empowering each other to reach their full potential and pursue their dreams. Mothers play a vital role in supporting their daughters' ambitions, providing encouragement, guidance, and practical assistance along the way. Similarly, daughters can uplift their mothers, offering words of affirmation, appreciation, and encouragement to bolster their confidence and self-esteem. By lifting each other up and celebrating each other's successes, they create a dynamic of mutual empowerment that strengthens their bond.

3. **Emotional Support and Validation:** Central to a strong mother-daughter connection is the ability to provide

emotional support and validation to one another. Mothers offer a nurturing presence and a listening ear, offering comfort, empathy, and reassurance during times of difficulty or distress. Daughters, in turn, provide a source of emotional support for their mothers, offering understanding, empathy, and companionship in times of need. This reciprocal exchange of emotional support deepens their connection and fosters a sense of closeness and intimacy.

4. **Resilience in Adversity:** Building a strong mother-daughter connection involves weathering challenges and adversity together, emerging stronger and more resilient as a result. Mothers and daughters may face obstacles, setbacks, and hardships throughout their lives, but their bond provides a source of strength and resilience to navigate these challenges. By facing adversity together, supporting each other through difficult times, and finding strength in their shared connection, they cultivate resilience and fortitude that strengthens their relationship.

5. **Continuing Growth and Evolution:** A strong mother-daughter connection is not static but continues to grow and evolve over time. As both parties navigate the complexities of life, their relationship may undergo changes and transformations, adapting to new circumstances and challenges. By embracing change, fostering open communication, and remaining committed to nurturing their connection, mothers and daughters can navigate life's twists and turns with grace and resilience. Through ongoing growth and evolution, their bond deepens and matures, becoming an enduring source of love, support, and companionship for years to come.

Ultimately, building a strong and supportive mother-daughter connection requires effort, patience, and a willingness to prioritize the relationship. By fostering open communication, spending quality time together, showing appreciation and support, and respecting each other's boundaries, mothers and daughters can cultivate a deep and meaningful bond that withstands the test of time. Through mutual love, understanding, and commitment, they can build a relationship that enriches their lives and brings them closer together.

Chapter 10
Lessons from Motherhood
"Motherhood: all love begins and ends there."
- Robert Browning

Motherhood is a timeless journey that transcends borders, cultures, and generations. It is a journey filled with profound lessons, invaluable insights, and transformative experiences that shape individuals and societies in profound ways. From the tender moments of infancy to the trials and triumphs of adolescence and adulthood, mothers navigate the complexities of parenthood with unwavering love, resilience, and dedication. Along this journey, they impart wisdom, guidance, and inspiration that reverberate through the lives of their children and beyond.

In this chapter, we delve into the rich tapestry of lessons woven through the fabric of motherhood. From the timeless wisdom passed down through generations to the inspirational stories of maternal guidance and resilience, we explore the myriad ways in which motherhood serves as a beacon of light, illuminating the path to self-discovery, growth, and fulfillment. Through reflection, storytelling, and introspection, we uncover the profound impact of maternal influence on individuals, families, and societies as a whole, celebrating the enduring legacy of motherhood for generations to come.

Join us as we embark on a journey of exploration and discovery, delving into the lessons learned from the boundless love, sacrifice, and wisdom of mothers around the world. Through the lens of motherhood, we gain insights into the human experience, forging connections, and finding meaning in the shared joys and challenges of raising the next generation. As we navigate this chapter together, may we honor the remarkable journey of motherhood and the invaluable lessons it imparts to us all.

Wisdom and life lessons passed down from mothers to their children:

Throughout the ages, motherhood has been revered as a sacred journey, rich with timeless wisdom and profound insights that transcend the boundaries of time and space. From generation to generation, mothers have served as custodians of knowledge, passing down age-old traditions, values, and teachings to their children with love and reverence.

In the tapestry of maternal wisdom, mothers offer not only practical advice but also profound insights into the human experience. From the moment a child is cradled in their mother's arms, they are enveloped in a tapestry of wisdom woven through the fabric of maternal love. Through gentle lullabies whispered in the quiet of the night and stories shared by the fireside, mothers impart lessons that echo through the corridors of time. These teachings, rooted in the wisdom of countless generations, offer guidance and perspective that shape the way individuals perceive and navigate the world around them.

In the tender embrace of maternal love, children learn the importance of kindness, empathy, and resilience. They glean insights into the complexities of human relationships, the power of forgiveness, and the beauty of compassion. Moreover, the lessons passed down through generations serve as a bridge connecting the past, present, and future. Mothers, drawing from their own life experiences and the collective wisdom of their ancestors, impart invaluable lessons that transcend mere words, instilling in their children a sense of purpose, courage, and self-belief.

From generation to generation, mothers have served as custodians of knowledge, passing down age-old traditions, values, and teachings to their children with love and reverence. As children learn from the experiences and teachings of their mothers, they become stewards of a rich legacy, entrusted with preserving and perpetuating the wisdom of their forebears. These stories of triumph over adversity, resilience in the face of hardship, and the enduring power of love to heal and transform become a living testament to the enduring legacy of maternal love and wisdom, honoring the sacrifices and struggles of those who came before them. Through these narratives, children glean not only knowledge but also a deeper understanding of their own capacity for growth and resilience, carrying forth the torch of knowledge and understanding into a world that is constantly evolving.

Inspirational Stories of Maternal Guidance:

- *A Mother's Unyielding Devotion:* At the heart of every inspirational story of maternal guidance lies a mother's unyielding devotion to her children. Despite facing formidable challenges and obstacles, mothers persevere with unwavering determination and love. Their steadfast commitment to their children's well-being inspires admiration and respect, showcasing the extraordinary lengths to which a mother will go to ensure the happiness and success of her family. Through their actions and sacrifices, mothers demonstrate the transformative power of unconditional love, leaving an indelible mark on the lives of those they cherish.
- *The Courage to Confront Adversity:* In the face of adversity, mothers display remarkable courage and resilience, serving as powerful role models for perseverance and strength. Whether overcoming personal hardships, navigating difficult circumstances, or advocating for their children's rights, mothers demonstrate an unwavering resolve to confront challenges head-on. Their ability to remain steadfast in the

face of adversity inspires hope and instills confidence, showing that with determination and perseverance, even the most daunting obstacles can be overcome.

- ***Empowering Through Empathy:*** Mothers possess a unique capacity for empathy, allowing them to connect deeply with their children's emotions and experiences. Through their empathetic presence and understanding, mothers provide a source of comfort and support during times of uncertainty and distress. By validating their children's feelings and offering reassurance, mothers empower them to navigate life's ups and downs with resilience and grace. In doing so, they cultivate a sense of emotional intelligence and empathy within their children, fostering strong and nurturing relationships built on trust and understanding.

- ***Embracing Diversity and Inclusion:*** Mothers are champions of diversity and inclusion, fostering environments where every child feels valued and accepted for who they are. Through their actions and teachings, mothers instill in their children a deep appreciation for diversity, teaching them to celebrate differences and embrace the richness of cultural heritage. By nurturing environments of inclusivity and respect, mothers empower their children to become compassionate and empathetic individuals who contribute positively to a diverse society.

- ***Sacrifices for the Greater Good:*** Mothers exemplify the spirit of selflessness through their willingness to make sacrifices for the greater good of their families. Whether it's putting their own needs aside to prioritize their children's well-being, making financial sacrifices to provide opportunities for their children, or sacrificing personal aspirations for the sake of their family's success, mothers demonstrate a profound dedication to the welfare of their loved ones. Their acts of sacrifice serve as powerful examples of love in action, inspiring others to prioritize compassion and generosity in their own lives.

- *Advocates for Justice and Equality:* Mothers are tireless advocates for justice and equality, advocating for the rights and dignity of all individuals, especially marginalized and underserved communities. Whether fighting for gender equality, racial justice, or social equity, mothers use their voices and platforms to challenge injustice and create a more equitable world for future generations. Through their advocacy and activism, mothers model the importance of standing up for what is right and taking action to effect positive change, leaving a legacy of empowerment and social progress for their children to carry forward.

- *Nurturing Creativity and Imagination:* Mothers cultivate a sense of wonder and creativity in their children, encouraging them to explore their passions and pursue their dreams. Through activities such as storytelling, arts and crafts, and imaginative play, mothers inspire their children to think creatively, problem-solve, and express themselves authentically. By fostering environments that nurture curiosity and imagination, mothers ignite a lifelong love of learning and creativity in their children, empowering them to embrace their unique talents and pursue their aspirations with confidence and enthusiasm.

- *Cultivating Environmental Stewardship:* Mothers are stewards of the environment, teaching their children the importance of sustainability, conservation, and environmental responsibility. Through their actions and teachings, mothers instill in their children a deep respect for nature and a sense of responsibility to protect the planet for future generations. Whether through recycling, reducing waste, or participating in conservation efforts, mothers demonstrate the significance of caring for the Earth and leaving a positive impact on the world. By instilling values of environmental stewardship, mothers empower their children to become conscientious global citizens who strive to create a more sustainable and harmonious world.

Reflecting on the Impact of a Mother's Influence:

The influence of a mother extends far beyond the bounds of familial relationships, shaping the very fabric of society and leaving an indelible mark on the lives of individuals and communities. From the tender embrace of infancy to the guiding hand of adulthood, mothers play a pivotal role in nurturing, guiding, and inspiring their children to reach their fullest potential.

At the heart of a mother's influence lies a boundless wellspring of love, compassion, and wisdom. It is a love that knows no bounds, transcending distance, time, and circumstance to envelop her children in its warm embrace. Through her unwavering support and encouragement, a mother instills within her children a sense of confidence, resilience, and self-belief that serves as a guiding light through life's trials and triumphs.

Moreover, a mother's influence extends beyond the realm of personal development, shaping the very foundation of society through her values, beliefs, and actions. From instilling principles of kindness, empathy, and integrity to advocating for justice, equality, and social change, mothers serve as powerful agents of transformation in their communities and beyond.

Through their words and deeds, mothers impart invaluable lessons and insights that echo through the corridors of time, shaping the destinies of future generations. Whether through the timeless wisdom passed down through generations, the selfless sacrifices made for the sake of their families, or the unwavering advocacy for a more just and equitable world, mothers leave an enduring legacy that reverberates through the ages.

In the quiet moments of reflection, we come to realize the depth of a mother's influence—the quiet strength that steadies us in times of uncertainty, the gentle guidance that illuminates our path, and the boundless love that knows no limits. It is in the whispered words of encouragement, the comforting embrace during moments of sorrow, and the unwavering belief in our potential that we find solace and inspiration. A mother's influence transcends the ordinary, shaping our character, nurturing our spirit, and instilling within us the values that guide us through life's journey. It is a legacy of love that we carry within our hearts, a beacon of hope that lights our way, and a testament to the enduring power of a mother's love to transform lives and touch the soul.

As we reflect on the profound impact of a mother's influence, let us honor and celebrate the immeasurable contributions of mothers everywhere. May we carry forth their teachings with gratitude and humility, embodying the spirit of love, compassion, and resilience that defines the essence of motherhood.

Learning from the Challenges and Joys of Motherhood:

Motherhood is a profound journey marked by a tapestry of experiences, from the trials that test our resolve to the moments of pure joy that fill our hearts with warmth. In the sleepless nights of infancy, mothers discover the boundless depths of their resilience, finding strength in the midst of exhaustion and uncertainty. Through the milestones of childhood, they witness the transformative power of love and patience, as they nurture and guide their children through each new discovery and triumph. And in the trials of adolescence, mothers confront their own vulnerabilities and imperfections, learning the art of forgiveness and grace as they navigate the turbulent waters of parenthood.

Yet, amidst the challenges and chaos, there are moments of profound joy and fulfillment that serve as reminders of the beauty and wonder of motherhood. It is in the first flutter of a newborn's heartbeat, the infectious laughter of a child at play, and the quiet moments of connection shared between mother and child that the true essence of motherhood is revealed. These moments, though fleeting, are etched into the fabric of our memories, serving as beacons of light that guide us through the darkest of days.

Through the highs and lows of motherhood, individuals are invited to embark on a journey of self-discovery and growth, where each challenge becomes an opportunity for learning and reflection. It is in the moments of vulnerability and doubt that mothers discover the depths of their strength, courage, and resilience. And it is in the moments of joy and triumph that they find solace and fulfillment, knowing that their sacrifices are not in vain.

In embracing the lessons inherent in both the struggles and triumphs of motherhood, individuals gain a deeper understanding of themselves and the world around them. They learn to appreciate the beauty of imperfection, the value of perseverance, and the transformative power of love. And in doing so, they honor the sacred journey of motherhood, embracing its challenges and joys with open hearts and grateful spirits.

Amidst the chaos and uncertainty of motherhood, there exists a profound beauty—a beauty born from the depths of sacrifice, resilience, and unwavering love. It is in the quiet moments of tenderness, the shared laughter echoing through the halls, and the unspoken bonds that transcend words, where the true essence of motherhood is revealed. Through every tear wiped away, every scraped knee kissed, and every dream whispered in the night, mothers weave a tapestry of love that stretches across generations, binding hearts and souls in an eternal embrace. In the midst of life's storms, it is the warmth of a mother's love that serves as a beacon of hope, guiding us through the darkest nights and illuminating the path toward brighter tomorrows. Truly, the journey of motherhood is a testament to the resilience of the human spirit and the boundless capacity of the heart to love, nurture, and heal.

Embracing the Transformative Power of Motherhood:

At its core, motherhood is a sacred journey of self-discovery and transformation, where individuals are called upon to tap into reservoirs of strength, resilience, and unconditional love they never knew existed. Through the nurturing embrace of a child, mothers embark on a profound voyage of personal growth and evolution that reverberates through every aspect of their being. This transformation is not confined to the realm of parenthood but extends far beyond, shaping how individuals perceive themselves and interact with the world around them.

In the tender moments of late-night feedings and soothing lullabies, mothers uncover depths of patience and compassion they never thought possible. They learn to navigate the complexities of parenthood with grace and humility, embracing the inherent challenges as opportunities for growth and self-reflection. Through the joys and sorrows of motherhood, individuals are transformed, emerging stronger, wiser, and more resilient than they ever imagined.

This transformation is not only a personal journey but also a ripple effect that touches the lives of those around them. By embodying the virtues of empathy, compassion, and selflessness, mothers inspire others to embrace the transformative power of love and kindness. They become beacons of light in a world often shrouded in darkness, illuminating the path toward a more compassionate and interconnected society.

As individuals embrace the transformative power of motherhood, they unlock new depths of empathy, compassion, and self-awareness within themselves. They learn to embrace the beauty of imperfection, the value of vulnerability, and the profound impact of unconditional love. In doing so, they enrich not only their own lives but also the lives of those they touch, leaving an indelible mark on the world that transcends time and space.

In conclusion, motherhood is a transformative journey that shapes individuals in profound ways, unlocking new depths of strength, resilience, and unconditional love. Through the joys and challenges of nurturing a child, mothers discover the transformative power of empathy, compassion, and self-awareness, enriching their lives and the lives of those around them. As we embrace the transformative essence of motherhood, we are reminded of its enduring impact on shaping our identities and influencing our journey through life. Let us honor and celebrate the transformative power of motherhood, recognizing it as a sacred journey of self-discovery and personal growth.

Chapter 11
Balancing Motherhood and Career
"You can have it all. You just can't have it all at once."
- Oprah Winfrey

In the intricate dance of life, mothers often find themselves navigating the delicate balance between nurturing their families and pursuing their professional aspirations. The journey of balancing motherhood and career is a multifaceted one, marked by triumphs, challenges, and poignant moments of self-discovery. In this chapter, we embark on a heartfelt exploration of the intricate tapestry that weaves together the roles of motherhood and career, delving into the challenges faced by working mothers, the strategies employed to find harmony amidst the chaos, and the profound lessons learned along the way. Join us as we embark on a journey of empowerment, resilience, and unwavering determination to create a life that honors both the professional and maternal dimensions of our existence.

Challenges and strategies for working mothers:

Navigating the intricate balance between career and motherhood presents a myriad of challenges for working mothers, each requiring a unique blend of resilience, creativity, and resourcefulness to overcome. From the relentless demands of the workplace to the cherished responsibilities of caring for a family, working mothers often find themselves caught in a delicate balancing act, striving to excel in both domains while juggling the competing demands of time and energy.

One of the foremost challenges faced by working mothers is the struggle to manage competing priorities effectively. Balancing the demands of a demanding career with the needs of a growing family can often feel like an uphill battle, with deadlines looming, meetings to attend, and children to care for. The relentless pace of modern life can leave working mothers feeling stretched thin, constantly torn between professional obligations and familial responsibilities.

Moreover, working mothers often grapple with feelings of guilt and self-doubt as they navigate the complexities of balancing career aspirations with the desire to be present for their families. The societal pressure to excel in both realms can weigh heavily on working mothers, leaving them feeling torn between the expectations of their employers and the needs of their loved ones.

Despite these challenges, working mothers employ a myriad of strategies to navigate the intricate balance between career and motherhood with grace and resilience. From establishing clear boundaries and priorities to leveraging technology and flexible work arrangements, working mothers find innovative ways to carve out space for both their professional and familial roles.

Moreover, working mothers often draw strength and support from their networks, whether it be through the solidarity of fellow working mothers or the unwavering support of family and friends. By fostering a sense of community and mutual support, working mothers create a supportive ecosystem that empowers them to thrive in both their personal and professional lives.

In the face of adversity, working mothers exemplify the power of resilience, determination, and unwavering dedication to creating a life that honors both their professional ambitions and their maternal instincts. Through their courage and perseverance, working mothers inspire us all to embrace the challenges of balancing career and motherhood with grace, resilience, and unwavering determination.

Challenges and strategies for working mothers:

Navigating the delicate balance between career and motherhood presents a myriad of challenges for working mothers, requiring them to employ strategic approaches and resilience to overcome these obstacles.

One significant challenge is the constant juggling act between professional responsibilities and the demands of family life. From managing deadlines and meetings at work to attending to the needs of children at home, working mothers often find themselves stretched thin, grappling with the pressure to excel in both domains.

Another challenge faced by working mothers is the struggle to overcome societal expectations and stereotypes surrounding gender roles. Despite advancements in gender equality, many working mothers still encounter bias and judgment, both in the workplace and within their communities. The pressure to conform to traditional gender norms while pursuing a career can create feelings of guilt and inadequacy, adding an additional layer of complexity to the balancing act.

Moreover, working mothers often contend with the elusive quest for work-life balance. The blurred boundaries between work and home life, compounded by the ever-increasing demands of modern-day careers, can leave working mothers feeling overwhelmed and burnt out. Striking a harmonious equilibrium between professional success and personal fulfillment requires careful planning, boundary-setting, and self-care practices.

Despite these challenges, working mothers employ various strategies to navigate the complexities of balancing career and motherhood effectively. One such strategy is prioritization, wherein working mothers identify their core values and allocate their time and energy accordingly. By focusing on tasks and activities that align with their priorities, working mothers can optimize their productivity and maintain a sense of balance amidst competing demands.

Additionally, working mothers often leverage support systems and resources to alleviate the burden of caregiving responsibilities. This may involve enlisting the help of family members, hiring childcare services, or collaborating with supportive partners to share household and parenting duties. By delegating tasks and seeking assistance when needed, working mothers can create space for professional growth and personal fulfillment.

Furthermore, flexible work arrangements and remote work options have emerged as valuable tools for working mothers seeking to achieve greater flexibility and autonomy in their careers. By negotiating flexible schedules, telecommuting opportunities, or alternative work arrangements with employers, working mothers can better accommodate their caregiving responsibilities while maintaining their professional aspirations.

In essence, while the challenges of balancing career and motherhood may seem daunting, working mothers demonstrate remarkable resilience and resourcefulness in overcoming these obstacles. By employing strategic approaches, leveraging support systems, and advocating for greater flexibility in the workplace, working mothers pave the way for a more inclusive and equitable future, where women can thrive both personally and professionally.

Overcoming guilt and societal expectations:

Overcoming feelings of guilt and societal expectations is a significant hurdle that many working mothers encounter on their journey to balance career and motherhood. Society often imposes unrealistic standards and expectations on women, perpetuating the myth of the "perfect" mother who effortlessly manages both professional and familial responsibilities without faltering. This idealized image can create immense pressure and feelings of inadequacy for working mothers, leading to pervasive guilt and self-doubt.

One common source of guilt for working mothers is the perceived notion that they are neglecting their children by pursuing a career outside the home. Despite evidence to the contrary, societal norms often dictate that a mother's primary role should be that of a caregiver, placing undue pressure on women to prioritize family over career aspirations. This internalized guilt can erode confidence and hinder professional advancement, as working mothers grapple with the belief that they are failing to meet societal expectations of motherhood.

Moreover, working mothers may experience guilt over perceived shortcomings in their parenting, such as missing important milestones or not being present for every moment of their children's lives. The relentless pursuit of work-life balance can leave working mothers feeling torn between competing priorities, struggling to reconcile their professional ambitions with their desire to be fully present for their families. This internal conflict can exacerbate feelings of guilt and self-blame, perpetuating a cycle of negative self-talk and emotional distress.

To overcome feelings of guilt and societal expectations, working mothers must challenge the myth of the "perfect" mother and embrace the reality of their own unique circumstances. This involves reframing self-defeating beliefs and adopting a more compassionate and realistic perspective on motherhood and career success. By acknowledging that perfection is unattainable and that imperfection is a natural part of the human experience, working mothers can cultivate self-acceptance and resilience in the face of societal pressures.

Additionally, seeking support from fellow working mothers, mentors, or mental health professionals can provide valuable reassurance and guidance in navigating feelings of guilt and societal expectations. Sharing experiences and insights with others who understand the challenges of balancing career and motherhood can foster a sense of solidarity and empowerment, reminding working mothers that they are not alone in their struggles.

Furthermore, practicing self-care and setting boundaries are essential strategies for combating feelings of guilt and maintaining emotional well-being. By prioritizing time for rest, relaxation, and self-reflection, working mothers can replenish their energy reserves and cultivate a sense of balance in their lives. Setting realistic expectations and boundaries in both professional and personal spheres enables working mothers to protect their mental and emotional health while pursuing their goals and aspirations.

Overcoming guilt and societal expectations requires a commitment to self-compassion, self-care, and self-empowerment. By challenging societal norms, seeking support, and prioritizing personal well-being, working mothers can navigate the complexities of balancing career and motherhood with grace and resilience, paving the way for greater fulfillment and success in all aspects of their lives.

In addition to the challenges and strategies outlined above, it's important to acknowledge the role of workplace policies and cultural attitudes in supporting working mothers. Employers play a crucial role in creating a supportive work environment that accommodates the needs of working mothers, such as flexible work arrangements, paid parental leave, and on-site childcare facilities. By implementing family-friendly policies and fostering a culture of inclusivity and support, organizations can empower working mothers to thrive in both their professional and personal lives.

Furthermore, promoting gender equality and challenging traditional gender roles is essential for dismantling societal expectations that place undue burden on working mothers. By advocating for equal opportunities and representation in the workplace, society can create a more equitable and inclusive environment where women are valued for their contributions both inside and outside the home. This shift towards gender parity benefits not only working mothers but also future generations, paving the way for a more just and equitable society for all.

In conclusion, balancing motherhood and career is a multifaceted journey filled with challenges, triumphs, and personal growth. Working mothers face a myriad of obstacles as they strive to excel in both their professional and familial roles, from navigating workplace demands to managing household responsibilities. However, through resilience, determination, and the support of their communities, working mothers can overcome these challenges and find fulfillment in both spheres of their lives. It's essential to recognize the importance of workplace policies, cultural attitudes, and societal expectations in supporting working mothers and fostering gender equality. By advocating for inclusive practices and challenging traditional gender roles, we can create a more equitable and supportive environment where working mothers can thrive. Ultimately, the journey of balancing motherhood and career is a testament to the strength, resilience, and unwavering dedication of women everywhere.

Chapter 12
The Evolution of Motherhood

"Motherhood has evolved over time, but the essence of maternal love remains constant."

- Unknown

Throughout history, the concept of motherhood has undergone significant evolution, reflecting the dynamic interplay of cultural, social, and economic forces. From ancient civilizations to modern societies, the roles and expectations placed on mothers have shifted in response to changing norms, values, and technological advancements. In this chapter, we will explore the historical perspectives on motherhood, tracing its evolution from antiquity to the present day. We will delve into the changing roles and expectations of mothers over time, examining how societal attitudes and cultural beliefs have shaped the experiences of motherhood. Additionally, we will discuss the modern challenges and opportunities facing mothers in today's fast-paced and interconnected world. Through this exploration, we aim to gain a deeper understanding of the complexities and nuances inherent in the timeless institution of motherhood.

Historical perspectives on motherhood:

Historical perspectives on motherhood provide invaluable insights into the cultural, social, and religious contexts that have shaped the roles and expectations of mothers throughout different epochs. In ancient civilizations such as Mesopotamia, Egypt, and Greece, motherhood was often revered and celebrated, with goddesses like Isis and Demeter symbolizing fertility, nurturing, and protection. Mothers were regarded as primary caregivers and educators, responsible for instilling moral values, traditions, and skills in their children.

During the Middle Ages in Europe, motherhood was deeply intertwined with religious beliefs and practices, as Christianity emphasized the virtues of maternal piety, sacrifice, and devotion. Mothers were expected to raise children in accordance with Christian teachings, imparting lessons of faith, obedience, and humility. However, motherhood was also shaped by socioeconomic factors, with peasant women facing the dual burdens of agricultural labor and child-rearing, while noblewomen focused on managing households and transmitting aristocratic values to their offspring.

The Renaissance period witnessed a shift in attitudes towards motherhood, as humanist ideals emphasized the importance of education and intellectual development. Mothers were encouraged to play an active role in their children's upbringing, fostering curiosity, creativity, and critical thinking. However, societal expectations of motherhood remained largely patriarchal, with women's roles confined to the domestic sphere and subordinate to those of men.

The Industrial Revolution brought about profound changes in the nature of motherhood, as urbanization and industrialization reshaped family dynamics and gender roles. Working-class mothers faced the challenges of factory labor and urban poverty, often struggling to balance employment with childcare responsibilities. Meanwhile, middle-class mothers embraced the ideals of domesticity and maternal nurture, constructing the image of the "angel in the house" who devoted herself entirely to the care and upbringing of her children.

In the 20th century, the rise of feminism and women's rights movements sparked a reevaluation of traditional gender roles and expectations. Mothers increasingly entered the workforce in greater numbers, challenging the notion that their sole role was to be homemakers and caregivers. The advent of contraception and reproductive rights empowered women to control their fertility and make choices about motherhood on their own terms.

Today, motherhood is characterized by diversity and complexity, reflecting the myriad ways in which women navigate the competing demands of work, family, and personal fulfillment. While some mothers choose to prioritize their careers, others opt for more traditional roles as stay-at-home parents. Regardless of their choices, mothers continue to play a vital role in shaping the lives of their children and contributing to the fabric of society, embodying the enduring ideals of love, sacrifice, and resilience that have defined motherhood throughout history.

Changing roles and expectations of mothers over time:

The roles and expectations of mothers have undergone significant evolution over time, reflecting shifts in societal norms, economic conditions, and cultural values. From ancient civilizations to the modern era, mothers have adapted to changing circumstances while navigating the complexities of maternal responsibility, identity, and fulfillment.

In ancient societies, mothers were primarily tasked with the care and upbringing of children, as well as the management of household affairs. Their roles were deeply entrenched in cultural and religious traditions, with expectations of maternal piety, obedience, and devotion. Motherhood was revered and celebrated, yet women's autonomy and agency were often limited by patriarchal structures and societal norms.

During the Middle Ages and Renaissance, motherhood continued to be revered within the context of religious and familial duties. Mothers were expected to embody virtues such as selflessness, humility, and moral guidance, instilling religious beliefs and societal values in their children. However, socioeconomic factors such as class and status influenced the roles and responsibilities of mothers, with noblewomen often focused on managing estates and raising heirs, while peasant women balanced agricultural labor with childcare.

The Industrial Revolution brought about profound changes in the roles of mothers, as urbanization and industrialization reshaped family dynamics and labor patterns. Working-class mothers faced the dual burdens of factory work and childcare, often relying on extended family networks and community support to meet their familial obligations. Meanwhile, middle-class mothers embraced the ideals of domesticity and maternal nurture, overseeing the upbringing of their children while maintaining households.

In the 20th century, the rise of feminism and women's liberation movements challenged traditional notions of motherhood and gender roles. Mothers increasingly entered the workforce in response to economic necessity and aspirations for personal fulfillment and independence. The advent of contraception and reproductive rights provided women with greater control over their fertility and family planning decisions, enabling them to pursue education, careers, and other interests outside of motherhood.

Today, the roles of mothers are diverse and multifaceted, reflecting the intersection of individual choice, cultural expectations, and societal progress. While some mothers choose to prioritize their careers and pursue professional success, others opt for more traditional roles as primary caregivers and homemakers. Moreover, the rise of co-parenting and shared household responsibilities has challenged traditional gender roles, fostering greater equality and collaboration between parents in raising children.

Overall, the changing roles and expectations of mothers over time reflect broader shifts in society towards greater gender equality, individual autonomy, and diversity of choices. Despite these changes, the fundamental ideals of love, nurture, and sacrifice remain central to the concept of motherhood, transcending time and cultural boundaries.

Modern challenges and opportunities for mothers:

In the modern era, mothers face a myriad of challenges and opportunities as they navigate the complexities of balancing family responsibilities, career aspirations, and personal fulfillment. While advancements in technology, education, and women's rights have expanded opportunities for mothers in various spheres of life, they have also introduced new challenges and pressures unique to the contemporary world.

One of the most prominent challenges for modern mothers is achieving a work-life balance in an increasingly fast-paced and demanding society. Balancing the demands of a career with the needs of children and family can often feel like an uphill battle, leading to feelings of stress, guilt, and exhaustion. The rise of remote work and flexible scheduling options has provided some relief for mothers, allowing them to better juggle their professional and personal lives. However, the blurred boundaries between work and home life in the digital age can also exacerbate feelings of burnout and overwhelm.

Another significant challenge for modern mothers is the pressure to meet societal expectations of motherhood, which often idealize notions of perfection and sacrifice. From social media portrayals of "supermom" lifestyles to cultural narratives that equate maternal success with selflessness and martyrdom, mothers are bombarded with unrealistic standards that can undermine their sense of confidence and well-being. Moreover, the prevalence of "mom-shaming" and judgmental attitudes towards mothers' choices and parenting styles can further exacerbate feelings of inadequacy and insecurity.

In addition to these challenges, modern mothers also grapple with economic pressures, childcare costs, and access to supportive resources and services. The rising cost of living, stagnant wages, and limited access to affordable healthcare and childcare can place significant financial strain on families, particularly single mothers and those from marginalized communities. Moreover, the lack of paid parental leave policies and workplace support for mothers can hinder their ability to advance in their careers and achieve economic stability.

Despite these challenges, modern mothers also have access to unprecedented opportunities for personal growth, professional advancement, and community support. The proliferation of online parenting forums, support groups, and resources has created virtual communities where mothers can connect, share experiences, and seek advice from peers facing similar challenges. Moreover, the increasing visibility of diverse representations of motherhood in media and popular culture has helped challenge stereotypes and foster greater inclusivity and acceptance of different parenting styles and family structures.

Furthermore, advancements in technology and globalization have opened up new avenues for mothers to pursue education, entrepreneurship, and creative endeavors from the comfort of their homes. The rise of the gig economy and freelance opportunities has provided flexible income-generating options for mothers looking to supplement their household finances while maintaining autonomy over their schedules. Additionally, the growing emphasis on work-life integration and holistic well-being in corporate culture has led to greater recognition of the value of family-friendly policies and initiatives that support mothers in the workforce.

In conclusion, modern motherhood is characterized by a complex interplay of challenges and opportunities shaped by societal, economic, and technological forces. While mothers continue to navigate the pressures of balancing work and family life, they also possess resilience, resourcefulness, and a deep wellspring of love and determination that enable them to overcome obstacles and thrive in the face of adversity. By fostering supportive communities, advocating for inclusive policies, and embracing a diversity of experiences and perspectives, society can create a more equitable and empowering environment for mothers to flourish and fulfill their potential.

Chapter 13
The Legacy of a Mother's Love
"A mother's love is the fuel that enables a normal human being to do the impossible."
- Marion C. Garretty

In the tapestry of human existence, the love of a mother weaves a timeless thread that transcends generations, leaving an indelible mark on the hearts and souls of her descendants. Chapter 13 delves into the profound legacy of a mother's love, exploring how its essence reverberates through the corridors of time, shaping the destinies of families and communities. From the cherished traditions passed down through the ages to the enduring values and memories etched in the annals of history, the legacy of maternal love endures as a beacon of light, guiding future generations with its timeless wisdom and boundless compassion.

How a mother's love lives on through generations:

A mother's love is a timeless gift that transcends the boundaries of time and space, leaving an enduring legacy that echoes through the generations. From the tender embrace of a mother's arms to the gentle lullabies whispered in the night, the imprint of maternal love is etched into the very fabric of our being. As children grow and embark on their own life journeys, they carry with them the lessons and values instilled by their mothers, shaping their identities and guiding their actions.

Across cultures and continents, the bond between mother and child serves as a cornerstone of familial relationships, forging connections that span lifetimes. The love and guidance provided by mothers serve as a source of strength and inspiration, empowering their children to navigate life's challenges with courage and resilience. Even in the absence of physical presence, the spirit of a mother's love endures, a guiding light that illuminates the path forward for future generations.

Through stories, traditions, and cherished memories, the legacy of a mother's love is passed down from one generation to the next, enriching the lives of all who are touched by its grace. Whether through simple acts of kindness or profound acts of sacrifice, the impact of maternal love reverberates through the ages, shaping the course of history and leaving an indelible mark on the world.

1. ***Cultural Traditions and Rituals:*** Across cultures and societies, mothers play a central role in passing down cultural traditions and rituals from one generation to the next. Whether it's celebrating holidays, observing religious ceremonies, or participating in family customs, these practices serve as tangible reminders of a mother's enduring love and influence. Through these traditions, children learn about their cultural heritage and identity, strengthening their connection to their roots and the generations that came before them.

2. ***Inherited Traits and Characteristics:*** Beyond the tangible expressions of love and care, a mother's influence can also be seen in the inherited traits and characteristics passed down through genetic lineage. From physical features to personality traits and mannerisms, children often bear traces of their mother's legacy, serving as a tangible reminder of her presence and influence in their lives. These shared traits become a source of connection and comfort, linking generations together in a continuum of love and belonging.

3. ***Memories and Shared Stories:*** As time passes and memories fade, the stories and anecdotes shared by mothers become cherished treasures passed down through generations. Whether it's recounting tales of childhood adventures,

imparting words of wisdom, or sharing family folklore, these stories serve as a bridge connecting past, present, and future. Through the retelling of these memories, children keep alive the spirit and essence of their mother's love, ensuring that her legacy endures for generations to come.

4. ***Educational and Professional Achievements:*** A mother's love extends beyond the confines of the home and into the realm of education and professional achievements. Through her guidance, support, and encouragement, children are empowered to pursue their dreams and aspirations, achieving success in their chosen paths. Whether it's earning academic accolades, pursuing career milestones, or making meaningful contributions to society, these achievements stand as a testament to a mother's unwavering belief in her children's potential and her dedication to their growth and development.

5. ***Spiritual and Emotional Connections:*** At a deeper level, a mother's love creates spiritual and emotional connections that transcend physical boundaries and lifetimes. It is a love that transcends space and time, binding mothers and children together in a bond that endures beyond the realms of the tangible world. Through this spiritual connection, mothers continue to guide and protect their children, offering comfort, solace, and strength in moments of need. It is a love that transcends death, living on in the hearts and souls of those touched by its profound and enduring power.

Passing down traditions, values, and memories:

Mothers play a pivotal role in passing down traditions, values, and memories that shape the legacy of their love through generations. Through the transmission of cultural heritage and identity, mothers ensure that their family's customs and traditions remain alive and vibrant. Whether it's celebrating cultural festivals, preparing traditional meals, or speaking native languages, these practices foster a sense of pride and connection to one's cultural roots, enriching the lives of future generations.

In addition to cultural traditions, mothers impart core values and beliefs that serve as the moral compass for their children and grandchildren. Through their words, actions, and teachings, mothers instill principles such as kindness, honesty, empathy, and resilience. These timeless values provide a guiding light for navigating life's challenges and making ethical decisions, ensuring that the legacy of a mother's love extends far beyond her own lifetime.

Family rituals and routines established by mothers create opportunities for bonding and creating lasting memories as a family. Whether it's weekly Sunday dinners, bedtime stories, or annual vacations, these rituals strengthen family bonds and reinforce the importance of spending quality time together. By upholding these cherished traditions, mothers provide a sense of continuity and stability that nurtures a strong sense of belonging within the family unit.

Alongside cultural traditions and family rituals, mothers pass down personal legacies and life lessons that reflect their unique experiences and wisdom. Through personal anecdotes, pearls of wisdom, and practical advice, mothers leave behind a wealth of knowledge and insights for their descendants. These lessons serve as invaluable resources, guiding and inspiring future generations as they navigate life's journey, ensuring that the legacy of a mother's love endures long after she is gone.

Perhaps the most enduring aspect of a mother's love is the emotional bond she shares with her children. This bond transcends words and actions, encompassing a deep and unconditional love that defies explanation. Through their unwavering support, encouragement, and affection, mothers bestow upon their children the intangible gifts of love, acceptance, and emotional security. This emotional connection forms the cornerstone of a mother's legacy, shaping the emotional well-being and happiness of her children for generations to come.

Preserving the essence of maternal love:

Preserving the essence of maternal love involves more than just passing down traditions and values; it encompasses the intangible aspects of a mother's love that resonate through time. It's about cherishing the memories, the laughter, and the tender moments shared between a mother and her children. These precious moments, captured in photographs, handwritten notes, and cherished mementos, serve as tangible reminders of a mother's enduring love and presence in the lives of her children.

Moreover, preserving the essence of maternal love involves honoring the legacy of mothers who have come before us. It's about recognizing the sacrifices they made, the challenges they overcame, and the unwavering devotion they showed to their families. By commemorating their stories and celebrating their achievements, we ensure that their legacy lives on in the hearts and minds of future generations.

Furthermore, preserving the essence of maternal love requires us to embody the same qualities of compassion, resilience, and selflessness that define the maternal bond. It's about carrying forward the values and principles instilled in us by our mothers and passing them on to our own children and grandchildren. In doing so, we honor the legacy of maternal love and continue the timeless tradition of nurturing and caring for those we hold dear.

Ultimately, preserving the essence of maternal love is a testament to the enduring power of a mother's influence on her children and the world around her. It's a commitment to upholding the values of love, compassion, and empathy that define the essence of motherhood. By embracing these qualities and cherishing the memories and traditions passed down to us, we ensure that the legacy of maternal love continues to inspire and uplift future generations for years to come.

In conclusion, the legacy of a mother's love transcends time and space, weaving its way through the tapestry of generations with an enduring grace and beauty. It is a legacy defined by selflessness, sacrifice, and unwavering devotion—a legacy that continues to inspire and uplift long after our mothers have passed on. As we reflect on the profound impact of maternal love in our lives, let us cherish the memories, honor the traditions, and preserve the essence of this timeless bond. Through our words, actions, and deeds, may we keep the flame of maternal love burning brightly, illuminating the path for future generations to follow. For in the legacy of a mother's love, we find solace, strength, and the eternal promise of a bond that knows no end.

Chapter 14
A Mother's Reflections

"A mother's arms are more comforting than anyone else's."
- Princess Diana

Chapter 14 of our exploration into the intricate world of motherhood invites you to embark on a deeply personal journey. Titled "A Mother's Reflections," this chapter delves into the heartfelt stories and reflections shared by mothers from all walks of life. Here, we uncover the raw emotions, cherished memories, and profound insights that illuminate the path of motherhood. Through moments of joy, sadness, and growth, these reflections offer a poignant glimpse into the complex tapestry of maternal experiences. Join us as we delve into the rich tapestry of motherhood, guided by the wisdom and authenticity of those who have traversed its winding roads.

Personal stories and reflections from mothers:

In this section, mothers from diverse backgrounds and experiences have graciously shared their personal stories and reflections, offering a glimpse into the multifaceted journey of motherhood. From the tender moments of holding their newborns for the first time to the challenges of navigating adolescence and beyond, these narratives capture the essence of maternal love in its purest form. Through their candid accounts, mothers explore the intricacies of bonding with their children, the joys of witnessing milestones, and the profound impact of motherhood on their own growth and self-discovery. These stories serve as a testament to the universal nature of motherhood, transcending cultural, social, and geographical boundaries to resonate with readers around the world.

Here are a few examples of personal stories and reflections from mothers:

1. *The Strength of a Mother (Sarah):*

Sarah's story is one of resilience and determination in the face of adversity. As a single mother of two young children, she found herself thrust into the daunting role of sole provider and caregiver after her divorce. Initially overwhelmed by the magnitude of her new responsibilities, Sarah struggled to balance the demands of work and parenting while grappling with feelings of loneliness and uncertainty.

Despite the challenges she faced, Sarah drew upon an inner reservoir of strength and resilience to navigate through the storm. She poured her heart and soul into providing a nurturing and stable environment for her children, determined to shield them from the upheaval of divorce. Through her unwavering love and devotion, Sarah became a pillar of strength for her children, offering them comfort, stability, and reassurance during a tumultuous time in their lives.

As Sarah journeyed through the ups and downs of single parenthood, she discovered a newfound sense of purpose and empowerment within herself. She learned to trust in her instincts, embrace her vulnerabilities, and lean on her support network for guidance and encouragement. Through the challenges she faced, Sarah emerged stronger and more resilient than ever before, a testament to the transformative power of a mother's love.

Sarah's story serves as an inspiration to mothers everywhere, reminding them of their inherent strength and resilience in the face of adversity. Her unwavering determination to provide a better life for her children exemplifies the depth of a mother's love and the boundless lengths to which she will go to protect and nurture her family. In Sarah's journey, we find a powerful testament to the strength of a mother's love and the indomitable spirit that lies within each and every one of us.

1. *A Mother's Sacrifice (Emily):*

Emily's story is one of profound love and sacrifice, illustrating the lengths to which a mother will go to ensure the well-being and happiness of her child. Emily, a devoted mother of three, faced the unimaginable challenge of caring for her youngest son, Jacob, who was diagnosed with a rare and debilitating illness at a young age.

Despite the overwhelming burden of medical treatments, hospital visits, and emotional turmoil, Emily remained steadfast in her commitment to Jacob's care. She dedicated countless hours to researching treatments, consulting with specialists, and advocating for her son's needs, determined to give him the best possible chance at a fulfilling life.

As Jacob's illness progressed, Emily found herself navigating the complexities of palliative care and end-of-life decisions, grappling with the heartbreaking reality that she may one day have to say goodbye to her beloved son. Through it all, Emily remained a beacon of strength and resilience, drawing upon her unwavering love and faith to guide her through the darkest of times.

In the face of adversity, Emily found solace in the precious moments of joy and connection she shared with Jacob. Whether it was reading his favorite bedtime story, sharing a laughter-filled picnic in the park, or simply holding him close in a warm embrace, Emily treasured each and every moment they spent together, cherishing the bond they shared as mother and son.

Through her unwavering love and sacrifice, Emily exemplified the true essence of motherhood—a selfless commitment to the well-being and happiness of her child above all else. Her courage, resilience, and boundless love serve as an inspiration to mothers everywhere, reminding us of the profound impact a mother's love can have on the lives of her children, even in the face of life's greatest challenges..

1. *Finding Joy in the Chaos (Maria):*

Maria's story is a testament to the resilience and strength of a mother in the face of adversity. As a single mother of two, Maria found herself navigating the challenges of raising her children on her own while also facing financial hardship and societal stigma.

Despite the obstacles she encountered, Maria remained determined to provide her children with the love, support, and opportunities they deserved. Working multiple jobs to make ends meet, she sacrificed her own comfort and well-being to ensure that her children had everything they needed to thrive.

Through her unwavering dedication and sacrifice, Maria instilled in her children the values of perseverance, resilience, and compassion. She taught them the importance of hard work, integrity, and kindness, serving as a role model and guiding light in their lives.

Despite the challenges they faced, Maria and her children found strength in their bond as a family. Together, they weathered life's storms, celebrating triumphs and supporting each other through setbacks with love and unwavering determination.

Maria's story serves as a powerful reminder of the transformative power of a mother's love and the resilience of the human spirit. Her unwavering commitment to her children's well-being and her ability to overcome adversity with grace and determination exemplify the true essence of motherhood—a selfless devotion to the ones we love, no matter the challenges we may face.

1. *Lessons Learned (Jennifer):*

Jennifer's journey as a mother was filled with both moments of joy and challenges that tested her resilience and patience. As a young mother, Jennifer often found herself overwhelmed by the demands of parenthood, struggling to balance the responsibilities of caring for her children with the pressures of work and personal aspirations.

Amidst the chaos of daily life, Jennifer learned a valuable lesson about the importance of prioritizing self-care and setting boundaries. She realized that in order to be the best mother she could be for her children, she needed to prioritize her own physical, emotional, and mental well-being. Through trial and error, Jennifer discovered the power of self-care practices such as regular exercise, mindfulness, and seeking support from friends and family.

As Jennifer embraced self-care, she noticed a positive shift in her overall well-being and her ability to parent with patience and compassion. By taking time to recharge and nurture herself, she found that she had more energy and resilience to handle the challenges of motherhood with grace and resilience.

Through her journey, Jennifer learned that self-care is not a luxury but a necessity for every mother. She realized that by prioritizing her own well-being, she was setting a powerful example for her children about the importance of self-love, balance, and resilience in life.

Jennifer's story serves as a reminder that motherhood is a journey of growth and learning, and that sometimes the most important lessons come from taking care of ourselves so that we can better care for others. Her journey of self-discovery and self-care serves as an inspiration for mothers everywhere to prioritize their own well-being and find balance amidst the demands of parenthood.

1. *Gratitude for Motherhood (Rebecca):*

Rebecca's journey as a mother was marked by unexpected challenges and profound growth, teaching her valuable lessons about resilience, love, and the strength of the human spirit. When Rebecca's youngest child was diagnosed with a rare medical condition, she found herself thrust into a whirlwind of doctor's appointments, treatments, and uncertainty.

Amidst the fear and uncertainty, Rebecca discovered a well of inner strength she never knew she possessed. She became her child's fiercest advocate, tirelessly researching treatment options, seeking out specialists, and advocating for the care and support her child needed. In the face of adversity, Rebecca found courage she never knew she had, drawing upon a deep well of love and determination to navigate the challenges of her child's illness.

Through the ups and downs of her child's medical journey, Rebecca learned the importance of resilience and perseverance. She discovered that even in the darkest of times, there is always hope and strength to be found. Rebecca's unwavering love and dedication to her child became a source of inspiration for her family and friends, demonstrating the incredible power of a mother's love to overcome even the greatest of obstacles.

As her child's condition stabilized and their family adjusted to their new normal, Rebecca reflected on the lessons she had learned along the way. She realized that while life may not always go according to plan, it is our response to adversity that defines us. Through her journey as a mother, Rebecca discovered the depth of her own resilience and the boundless capacity of a mother's love to conquer even the greatest of challenges.

Rebecca's story serves as a testament to the strength and resilience of mothers everywhere, reminding us that even in the face of adversity, love has the power to triumph over fear and uncertainty. Her journey is a testament to the transformative power of motherhood, and a reminder that with love, determination, and resilience, anything is possible.

These stories and reflections indeed provide valuable insights into the multifaceted journey of motherhood. Through the highs and lows, joys and challenges, mothers exhibit remarkable resilience, unwavering strength, and boundless love for their children. Each narrative highlights the unique experiences and emotions that shape a mother's journey, underscoring the profound impact of maternal love and devotion on both the individual and collective human experience. Together, these stories weave a rich tapestry of motherhood, celebrating the diverse experiences and unwavering commitment of mothers everywhere.

Moments of joy, sadness, and growth in motherhood:

Moments of joy, sadness, and growth in motherhood encapsulate the full spectrum of emotions and experiences that mothers encounter throughout their journey. From the exhilarating highs of witnessing their child's first steps to the bittersweet moments of letting go as they embark on their own path, motherhood is a rollercoaster of emotions. In moments of joy, mothers find solace and fulfillment in the unconditional love they share with their children, reveling in the simple pleasures of laughter, hugs, and shared experiences. Yet, alongside the joy, mothers also navigate moments of sadness, grappling with the challenges and uncertainties that come with the responsibility of nurturing and guiding a child. Whether it's comforting a crying newborn in the wee hours of the night or navigating the complexities of adolescence, mothers confront their own vulnerabilities and fears while striving to provide comfort and support to their children. Amidst the joys and sorrows, motherhood becomes a journey of growth and self-discovery, as mothers learn and evolve alongside their children. Through the trials and triumphs of parenthood, mothers uncover inner reserves of strength, resilience, and wisdom, emerging transformed and empowered by the transformative power of maternal love.

In moments of joy, mothers cherish the simple pleasures of parenthood—the infectious laughter of a child, the warmth of a hug, the sparkle of excitement in their eyes. These fleeting moments become cherished memories that fill a mother's heart with boundless love and gratitude, serving as reminders of the beauty and wonder of life itself. From celebrating milestones like graduations and weddings to everyday moments of togetherness, mothers find joy in the precious moments shared with their children, treasuring each memory as a testament to the enduring bond they share.

However, motherhood also encompasses moments of sadness and heartache, as mothers navigate the inevitable challenges and setbacks that come with raising children. Whether it's witnessing their child's struggles, facing unexpected obstacles, or grappling with their own doubts and insecurities, mothers confront moments of sorrow with courage and resilience. In these times of sadness, mothers draw strength from the deep well of love within their hearts, offering comfort and support to their children while navigating their own emotions with grace and compassion.

Yet, amidst the joys and sorrows, motherhood becomes a journey of growth and self-discovery, as mothers learn and evolve alongside their children. Through the trials and triumphs of parenthood, mothers uncover inner reserves of strength, resilience, and wisdom, emerging transformed and empowered by the transformative power of maternal love. With each challenge overcome and lesson learned, mothers emerge stronger, wiser, and more deeply connected to the essence of who they are and the legacy they leave behind.

In the end, motherhood is a tapestry woven with threads of joy, sadness, and growth, each moment contributing to the rich and complex tapestry of the maternal experience. As mothers navigate the highs and lows of parenthood, they find solace in the enduring love that binds them to their children, finding beauty and meaning in the shared journey of life together.

A Mother's Unwavering Love: Navigating Tragedy and Finding Hope:

In the dimly lit room, where shadows dance upon the walls like ghosts of the past, a mother sits alone, her heart heavy with a burden no parent should ever bear. Her hands tremble as she clutches a faded photograph, the faces of her children smiling back at her with innocence long lost. Tears blur her vision, each drop a testament to the anguish that consumes her soul.

For years, she poured her love and devotion into raising her children, nurturing them with tenderness and care. She watched with pride as they took their first steps, spoke their first words, and embarked on the journey of life with boundless enthusiasm. She dreamed of a future filled with promise and possibility, where her children would flourish and thrive, leaving their mark on the world in ways she could only imagine.

But now, those dreams lie shattered at her feet, broken beyond repair by the cruel hand of fate. Her children, once the embodiment of her hopes and aspirations, now stand accused of unspeakable crimes that defy comprehension. Their faces haunt her every waking moment, their laughter echoing in the empty corridors of her mind like a haunting melody.

Yet, amidst the darkness that threatens to engulf her, a flicker of light remains—a beacon of hope that refuses to be extinguished. For in the depths of her despair, the mother finds solace in the knowledge that she did everything she could to raise her children with love and integrity. She taught them right from wrong, instilled in them values of compassion and empathy, and prayed fervently that they would choose the path of goodness and righteousness.

And though the world may judge her harshly for the sins of her children, she knows in her heart that she is not to blame. For mothers never tell their children bad things; instead, they work tirelessly to nurture them into kind, compassionate individuals who contribute positively to their families, their communities, and their nation.

So, let this be a lesson to the children of tomorrow—to cherish the love and sacrifices of their mothers, to heed their guidance and wisdom, and to walk through life with humility, compassion, and grace. For in the end, it is the legacy of love that mothers leave behind that truly defines the essence of motherhood—a legacy that endures long after they are gone, lighting the way for generations to come.

Insights and lessons learned along the journey:

Throughout the rollercoaster ride of motherhood, there are invaluable insights and profound lessons waiting to be discovered at every turn. From the euphoria of holding a newborn in one's arms for the first time to the bittersweet moments of watching them spread their wings and fly, the journey of motherhood is a masterclass in love, resilience, and personal growth.

One of the most poignant lessons that mothers learn along the way is the art of letting go. As their children grow and embark on their own paths, mothers must learn to loosen their grip and allow them the freedom to explore, make mistakes, and forge their own identities. It's a delicate balance between nurturing and releasing, between holding on tight and allowing space for independence to blossom. Through this process, mothers discover the power of trust—trust in their children's abilities to navigate life's challenges, and trust in the unbreakable bond that connects them, no matter where their journeys may lead.

Another lesson that resonates deeply with mothers is the importance of self-care. In the whirlwind of caregiving, it's all too easy for mothers to prioritize the needs of their children and neglect their own well-being. Yet, they soon come to realize that they cannot pour from an empty cup—that by taking care of themselves, they are better equipped to care for their loved ones. Whether it's stealing moments of solitude for reflection, indulging in hobbies that bring joy, or simply asking for help when needed, mothers learn that self-care isn't selfish—it's essential for their own health and happiness, as well as for the well-being of their families.

Furthermore, motherhood teaches mothers the value of resilience in the face of adversity. From sleepless nights and endless tantrums to unforeseen challenges and heartbreaks, mothers encounter obstacles of all shapes and sizes on their journey. Yet, time and time again, they rise to the occasion with unwavering strength and determination, drawing upon reservoirs of courage they never knew they possessed. Through the trials and tribulations of motherhood, they discover that they are capable of weathering any storm, and that even in the darkest moments, there is always a glimmer of hope to guide them forward.

Moreover, mothers learn the profound lesson of forgiveness—not only forgiving others for their shortcomings, but also forgiving themselves for their perceived failures. Motherhood is fraught with moments of doubt and guilt, where mothers question whether they are doing enough, being enough, loving enough. Yet, in the end, they come to understand that they are human, fallible, and inherently imperfect—and that it is precisely their imperfections that make them the perfect mothers for their children. By embracing their flaws and extending grace to themselves, mothers model self-compassion and acceptance for their children, teaching them the invaluable lesson that they are worthy of love, regardless of their perceived shortcomings.

In the end, the journey of motherhood is not just about raising children—it's about raising oneself. Through the ups and downs, the joys and sorrows, mothers embark on a transformative journey of self-discovery and personal growth, emerging stronger, wiser, and more compassionate than they ever thought possible. And though the road may be long and challenging, the lessons learned along the way are nothing short of miraculous—testaments to the enduring power of a mother's love to shape hearts, minds, and souls for generations to come.

Chapter 15
Forever Grateful

"A mother's love is patient and forgiving when all others are forsaking."
- Unknown

In the tapestry of life, there exists a thread of unconditional love that weaves its way through every moment, every triumph, and every trial. It is the thread of maternal love—a boundless, enduring force that shapes our existence in profound and immeasurable ways. As we embark on the final chapter of this journey, we pause to reflect on the remarkable gift of motherhood and express our heartfelt gratitude for the mothers who have touched our lives with their unwavering love and sacrifice.

From the moment we are cradled in our mother's arms, we are enveloped in a love that knows no bounds—a love that is as infinite as the universe and as timeless as the stars. It is a love that nurtures, guides, and sustains us through life's myriad joys and sorrows, lifting us up when we falter and celebrating with us when we triumph. It is a love that transcends distance, time, and circumstance, forever binding us to the women who gave us life.

In this final chapter, we come together to honor the extraordinary mothers who have shaped our lives and celebrate the profound impact of maternal love on our journey. Through stories, reflections, and expressions of gratitude, we pay tribute to the women whose love has illuminated our path, inspired our hearts, and transformed our souls. Join us as we embark on a journey of remembrance, appreciation, and celebration—a journey that honors the timeless bond between mother and child, and the immeasurable depth of a mother's love.

Expressing gratitude and appreciation for mothers:

In the hustle and bustle of daily life, it's easy to overlook the quiet yet profound ways in which mothers enrich our lives. From the gentle caress of a mother's hand to the reassuring warmth of her embrace, every gesture is infused with love and intention, shaping our memories and nurturing our souls. As we reflect on the countless sacrifices and selfless acts of kindness that define motherhood, we are filled with an overwhelming sense of gratitude and appreciation for the women who have given us the gift of life and love.

There are no words grand enough to capture the depth of gratitude we feel for our mothers. They have been our rock in times of uncertainty, our guiding light in moments of darkness, and our staunchest supporters in the face of adversity. They have sacrificed their own desires and dreams to ensure our happiness and well-being, pouring their heart and soul into every aspect of our lives. Their unwavering love and boundless compassion have been a constant source of strength and inspiration, shaping the very fabric of our existence.

As we express our gratitude for our mothers, we also acknowledge the countless women who have served as maternal figures in our lives. Whether they are grandmothers, aunts, sisters, or mentors, these women have played an integral role in shaping who we are and who we aspire to be. Their love knows no bounds, extending beyond the confines of biology to encompass the full breadth of human connection and compassion.

In expressing our gratitude for mothers, we also recognize the sacrifices and challenges they have faced along the way. Motherhood is a journey filled with highs and lows, triumphs and setbacks, yet through it all, mothers persevere with grace and resilience. They embody the true essence of unconditional love, giving of themselves freely and unconditionally, without expectation of reward or recognition.

So, to all the mothers out there—past, present, and future—we say thank you. Thank you for your unwavering love, your boundless compassion, and your tireless devotion. Thank you for the countless sacrifices you have made and the countless blessings you have bestowed upon us. We are forever grateful for the gift of your love and the privilege of calling you our mother.

Maternal love is a force unlike any other, shaping our very existence from the moment we enter this world. It is a love that knows no bounds, transcending time and space to envelop us in its warm embrace, guiding us through life's ups and downs with unwavering grace and compassion. As we reflect on the impact of maternal love on our lives, we are humbled by its profound influence and grateful for the blessings it bestows upon us.

From our earliest days, maternal love forms the foundation upon which we build our sense of self and navigate the world around us. It is the gentle touch of a mother's hand and the soothing cadence of her voice that reassure us in times of distress, providing comfort and security when we need it most. It is through her unwavering support and encouragement that we find the courage to chase our dreams and overcome life's obstacles with resilience and determination.

Maternal love is a beacon of light that guides us through life's darkest moments, illuminating the path ahead with hope and optimism. It is the unconditional acceptance and unwavering belief in our potential that empowers us to embrace our true selves and live authentically, free from fear or judgment. It is through her steadfast love and unwavering presence that we find the strength to weather life's storms and emerge stronger, wiser, and more compassionate beings.

As we journey through life, the impact of maternal love continues to shape our experiences, relationships, and outlook on the world. It is the lessons learned at a mother's knee and the values instilled in us from a young age that guide our actions and inform our decisions. It is the memories of shared laughter and tears, triumphs and challenges, that bind us to our mothers in an unbreakable bond that transcends time and space.

In acknowledging the impact of maternal love on our lives, we are reminded of the countless ways in which our mothers have shaped who we are and who we aspire to be. Their love is a constant source of inspiration and guidance, guiding us through life's twists and turns with unwavering grace and compassion. It is a love that endures long after they are gone, a legacy that lives on in the hearts and minds of those they have touched along the way.

The bond between a mother and child is a sacred and enduring connection that transcends words and spans the depths of the human heart. It is a bond forged in the fires of love, nurtured through the tender moments of infancy and strengthened by the trials and triumphs of life's journey. As we celebrate this profound bond, we honor the countless ways in which it shapes our lives and enriches our souls.

At its core, the bond between a mother and child is rooted in love—a love that knows no limits and defies all boundaries. It is a love that is unconditional, unwavering, and eternal, transcending the passage of time and the challenges of life. It is a love that is as boundless as the heavens and as deep as the ocean, filling our hearts with warmth and light even in the darkest of times.

Through the bond between mother and child, we find solace in the knowledge that we are never alone, that we are forever connected to someone who loves us unconditionally and believes in us wholeheartedly. It is a bond that offers comfort in times of sorrow, strength in times of weakness, and hope in times of despair. It is a bond that reminds us of our inherent worth and potential, inspiring us to reach for the stars and pursue our dreams with courage and determination.

As we celebrate the enduring bond between mother and child, we pay tribute to the countless sacrifices and selfless acts of love that define this sacred relationship. We honor the mothers who have held us in their arms, wiped away our tears, and cheered us on every step of the way. We cherish the memories of shared laughter and joy, of whispered secrets and bedtime stories, knowing that these moments are etched forever in our hearts.

In celebrating the bond between mother and child, we recognize the profound impact it has on shaping who we are and who we aspire to be. It is a bond that teaches us the true meaning of love, compassion, and resilience, guiding us through life's ups and downs with unwavering grace and strength. It is a bond that reminds us of the power of connection and the beauty of unconditional love—a bond that will forever remain in our hearts, binding us together in a bond that transcends time and space.

Conclusion

In the tapestry of life, woven with threads of joy, sorrow, and resilience, one thread shines brighter than all others—the thread of unconditional love that binds a mother to her child. Through the twists and turns of life's journey, through moments of triumph and moments of despair, it is this unwavering love that sustains us, uplifts us, and carries us through the darkest of times.

As we reflect on the countless stories of sacrifice, strength, and unwavering devotion shared within these pages, we are reminded of the profound impact of maternal love on our lives. From the tender embrace of a mother's arms to the whispered words of encouragement that echo in our hearts, the love of a mother is a beacon of light that guides us through life's tumultuous waters, illuminating the path ahead with its boundless warmth and compassion.

In celebrating the journey of motherhood, we honor the resilience, grace, and selflessness of mothers everywhere. We pay tribute to the countless sacrifices made, the countless tears shed, and the countless dreams sacrificed on the altar of love. We recognize the indelible mark left by mothers on our lives, shaping who we are and who we aspire to be with their unwavering love and guidance.

As we turn the final page of this story, let us carry forth the lessons learned and the memories cherished, holding close to our hearts the enduring bond between mother and child. Let us express our gratitude and appreciation for the mothers who have touched our lives, shaping our destinies with their boundless love and unwavering support. And let us never forget the profound truth that it is love—the pure, unconditional love of a mother—that truly makes life worth living.

Dear Readers,

As we come to the end of this journey through the pages of "Unconditional Love: A Mother's Journey," I am filled with gratitude for each and every one of you who has joined us on this profound exploration of motherhood. Your support, your engagement, and your presence have made this journey all the more meaningful, and for that, I am truly thankful.

To all the mothers who have shared their stories, their wisdom, and their love, thank you for opening your hearts and allowing us to glimpse the beauty and complexity of the maternal experience. Your courage, your resilience, and your unwavering love inspire us all, and I am deeply grateful for the opportunity to celebrate your remarkable journey through these pages.

To the readers who have followed along with us, thank you for your curiosity, your compassion, and your willingness to engage with the stories and reflections shared within these chapters. Your presence has enriched this journey in ways that words cannot express, and I am humbled by your support and encouragement.

As we bid farewell to this chapter of our journey, I am excited to announce that new stories and adventures await us on the horizon. In the pages that lie ahead, we will continue to explore the timeless themes of love, resilience, and human connection, delving into the depths of the human experience with curiosity, compassion, and an open heart.

So, until we meet again on the next chapter of our journey, I extend my heartfelt thanks to each and every one of you for sharing in this beautiful exploration of motherhood. May the lessons learned, the memories cherished, and the bonds forged within these pages continue to inspire and uplift you on your own journey through life.

With deepest gratitude and warmest wishes,

B Pily (Pawhnai)

Don't miss out!

Visit the website below and you can sign up to receive emails whenever B Pily publishes a new book. There's no charge and no obligation.

https://books2read.com/r/B-A-NNBFB-OOXZC

BOOKS 2 READ

Connecting independent readers to independent writers.

Did you love *Unconditional Love: A Mother's Journey*? Then you should read *From Ideas to Enterprise*[1] by B Pily!

[2]

"From Idea to Enterprise: A Comprehensive Guide for Starting Your Own Business" by **B. Pily** is your essential roadmap to entrepreneurial success. Whether you're a first-time entrepreneur or a seasoned business owner, this comprehensive guide provides actionable strategies, expert advice, and real-world examples to help you navigate the journey of starting and growing a successful business from scratch.

Discover how to nurture your ideas into innovative concepts, secure funding, navigate legal and regulatory requirements, and cultivate a supportive network of mentors and peers. Learn essential techniques for managing finances effectively, delivering exceptional customer service, and leveraging technology to drive business growth.

---

1. https://books2read.com/u/3JLz6v

2. https://books2read.com/u/3JLz6v

With practical insights, personal anecdotes, and practical exercises, "From Idea to Enterprise" equips you with the knowledge and tools needed to turn your business dreams into reality. Whether you're launching a tech startup, a small retail business, or a creative venture, this book offers invaluable guidance on the path to entrepreneurial success.

Also by B Pily

From Ideas to Enterprise
Unconditional Love: A Mother's Journey

About the Author

B Pily is a passionate writer dedicated to exploring the complexities of human relationships, emotions, and experiences through storytelling. With a background in psychology and a keen interest in the intricacies of the human mind, B Pily infuses their writing with depth, authenticity, and empathy, creating characters and narratives that resonate with readers on a profound level.

Drawing inspiration from personal experiences, observations, and the world around them, B Pily delves into themes such as love, loss, resilience, and the pursuit of meaning and fulfillment. Through their work, they strive to offer readers a glimpse into the human condition, inviting them to reflect on their own lives and relationships with greater insight and understanding.

B Pily believes in the transformative power of literature to inspire, comfort, and provoke thought, and they are committed to creating stories that touch the hearts and minds of readers across the globe. Whether exploring the complexities of family dynamics, the nuances of romantic relationships, or the resilience of the human spirit, B Pily's writing seeks to illuminate the beauty and complexity of the human experience.